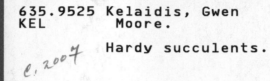

# HARDY SUCCULENTS

Tough Plants for Every Climate

# HARDY
# SUCCULENTS

GWEN MOORE KELAIDIS

PHOTOGRAPHY BY SAXON HOLT

Storey Publishing

Edited by Carleen Madigan Perkins and
    Gwen Steege

Art direction by Mary Winkelman Velgos

Cover design by Mary Winkelman Velgos
    based on a design by Chen Design
    Associates

Text design by Mary Winkelman Velgos
    based on a design by Chen Design
    Associates

Text production by Kristy L. MacWilliams

Illustrations by © Beverly Duncan

Indexed by Christine R. Lindemer,
    Boston Road Communications

Front cover: *Sempervivum* 'Faramir'

Front flap: *Agave parryi, Opuntia basilaris,
Sedum reflexum* 'Blue Spruce'

Back cover: *Yucca thompsoniana, Sedum
sieboldii* 'Mediovariegatum', *Delosperma*
'Kelaidis'

Back flap: *Escobaria missouriensis*

Page 2–3: *Agave neomexicana*

Page 6–7, left to right: *Orostachys spinosa,
Sempervivum* 'Gold Bug', *Agave parryi,
Opuntia engelmannii*

Text © Gwen Moore Kelaidis
Photography © Saxon Holt/Photo Botanic, except for the following:
© Karen Bussolini, page 88; © Scott Calhoun/Zona Gardens, pages 39, 52, 61, 83,
121 bottom right, and page 140; © Randy Tatroe, page 124

    The information in this book is true and complete to the best of our knowledge. All recom-
mendations are made without guarantee on the part of the author or Storey Publishing. The
author and publisher disclaim any liability in connection with the use of this information.
For additional information, please contact Storey Publishing, 210 MASS MoCA Way, North
Adams, MA 01247.

    Storey books are available for special premium and promotional uses and for customized
editions. For further information, please call 1-800-793-9396.

Printed in China by R.R. Donnelley
10 9 8 7 6 5 4 3 2 1

**Library of Congress Cataloging-in-Publication Data**

Kelaidis, Gwen Moore.
    Hardy succulents : tough plants for every climate / Gwen Moore Kelaidis.
        p.   cm.
    Includes index.
    ISBN 978-1-58017-700-9 (pbk. with flaps : alk. paper)
    ISBN 978-1-58017-701-6 (hardcover with jacket : alk. paper)
    1. Succulent plants.  I. Title.
SB438.K45 2008
635.9'525—dc22
                                                            2007039890

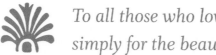

*To all those who love plants
simply for the beauty of their forms.*

## ACKNOWLEDGMENTS

*I would like to thank all of the following people, without whom this book would not have been possible: My parents, Ouida Agnes Johnston Moore and Jesse Carl Moore, for teaching me to garden carefully and lovingly. My botany professors, Dr. John Thomson and Dr. Hugh H. Iltis, and my teacher Dr. Theodore S. Cochrane, all of the University of Wisconsin, for opening up to me the natural world in all its devastating beauty and precious variety. My fellow gardeners, especially Panayoti Kelaidis, Kelly Grummons, and Bill Adams, for sharing freely their extensive knowledge of succulents and for their generous sharing of plants. Also Lauren Springer Ogden, Barbara Cochrane, and many more. That great plantsman and nurseryman Harlan Hamernik, of Bluebird Nursery in Clarkson, Nebraska, and his wife, Shirley, for their outrageously generous donations of plants for my gardens. My friends Sandy Snyder and Marcia Tatroe and my sister, Carla Ann Young, for their continual support and encouragement of this effort.*

—Gwen Moore Kelaidis

*In pursuit of photographs to illustrate this book, I must first thank my coauthor, Gwen, who kept me focused on the hardiness factor, even when I suggested hardiness issues in my Zone 9 garden prevented me from growing kalanchoe.*

*Acknowledgments to the gardeners, public gardens, and homeowners who so graciously allowed me access to their gardens are on page 148, but here I want to thank those who suggested locations and encouragement for this book: Panayoti Kelaidis of the Denver Botanic Gardens; Dan Benarcik at Chanticleer; Carlo Balistrieri; Ernesto Sandoval at the University of California, Davis; Richard Turner at Pacific Horticulture magazine; Carl Schoenfeld at Yucca Do Nursery; and Gwen Steege at Storey Publishing.*

*Finally, thanks, Flora!*

—Saxon Holt

# CONTENTS

# INTRODUCTION
# THE GLORIES OF SUCCULENCE

Succulents have a strong pull on our imagination. Their rounded, turgid nature appeals to us, just because they are so different from most other plants in our temperate universe. The succulents of the tropics and subtropics expand our concept of what a plant should look like, morphing like Proteus into endless and highly imaginative shapes and expressions. If a tomato plant or a marigold is an "average" plant of "average" shape with "average" leaves, succulents represent plant forms much farther out toward the extremes of the possible expression of the plant body.

The swollen leaves have a larger presence in space; their third dimension is simply larger than that of the average leaves of most flowering plants. And many are rounded in the way that the human body is rounded, reminding us of arms or the soft, touchable swell of a child's plump cheek.

Succulents are juicy inside, and although we don't often break them open or eat them, the promise of their wetness and water storage appeals to us. We are dependent on water, and finding it in our environment is pleasing. In the dry, windy prairies of Wyoming the low, tubby balls of *Coryphantha vivipara* are a strong contrast to the arid grasses. Because they can store water, we are confident they will endure through the years.

In the hot deserts of the Southwest, the stout, armed forms of yuccas and agaves are stalwarts of their ecosystems. They store water as if in anticipation of hard times to come, resolutely holding their own against the vagaries of erratic rainfall, the intensity of heat, and the driving force of dust storms. We admire their strength and tenacity, their seeming ability to foresee what is to come — although surely this is a case of natural selection, wherein only those that stored water survived.

In extremely desperate situations, succulents can actually provide life-giving fluids to people, whether it be a desert-crawler cutting open a barrel cactus to suck its inner pulp (how did he cut that thing open, anyway?) or adventurers grilling prickly pear pads to eat. But this is a book not about the utility of succulents to people, but rather concerning their contribution to the decorative art of gardening. How can we bring these unusual and charming plants into the daily lives of our garden, where we can share our world with them?

**LEFT:** The blue-green carpet of *Sedum reflexum* 'Blue Spruce' brilliantly complements the cool gray swords of *Agave parryi*.

**RIGHT:** Many cactus, like *Echinocereus reichenbachii,* are grown as much for their stunning blooms as for their structural presence.

## FORM, FUNCTION, AND FLOWERS

Many succulents are rosettes, holding their leaves close together on a foreshortened stem. Yuccas are an example — many species have no visible stem at all, although they have as many as 300 sword-shaped leaves. Hens-and-chicks (*Sempervivum*) boast very plump leaves arranged like an open and very double rose, forms into which one could look mesmerized for hours, a form that would challenge many an artist to draw but which reproduces itself effortlessly. Each new type of hens-and-chicks looks a bit different from the next, and all are endlessly fascinating because of their symmetry and varied arrangements of color.

Many succulents are also reliable citizens of the flower garden. Sedums, from *Sedum spurium* to *S. kamtschaticum* to *S. (Hylotelephium) spectabile* can be counted on to live on from year to year, whereas more exotic newcomers to the perennial border may perish after a single year or two. These succulents are hardworking and low-maintenance, suffering from few diseases and continuing to grow for many years even when ignored by the low-labor gardener, even when challenged by invading grass and encroaching neighbors.

Succulents can also protect us, our borders, and our gardens from intruders, whether with the sharp tips of agaves or the bright and barbed spines of cactus. There are many gardeners who rejoice in this aggressive-defensive quality, feeling their strength displayed in the garden. Are these gardeners managing their anger through plants? Or merely saving money on fences? Or simply relishing the diversity of the plant kingdom?

And then there are the flowers. Many hardy succulents have small, modest flowers, white or yellow, considered by some gardeners to be secondary to their lovely foliage, which is often stunning in its perfect symmetry. Some succulents indeed have soft and understated flowers, low clouds of white (*Sedum tartaricum*), or bright clouds of yellow, bringing sunshine down into the garden (cultivars of *Sedum middendorffianum,* for instance).

But succulents also seem to have a high proportion of the flashiest flowers of the Northern Hemisphere. Huge, glossy, shining flowers appear on the bodies of the humble cactus, the surprise of such sudden beauty astonishing and delighting us. A friend remarked that flowers on a normal plant are just flowers, but on a cactus they seem to be a miracle. Fanciers of cactus flowers are transported by the huge array of very large blooms that transform patches of prickly pears into exotic outdoor flower shops. Tiny ball cactus suddenly produce the most surprising displays of lovely flowers, like a gardenia or a full-blown rose suddenly pinned on a muted brown dress.

The humble, low mats of ice plant (*Delosperma*) foliage give rise to round, perfect flowers shining at ground level like bright new coins, flashing in the sun and blooming

over a long season. No flower can rival the glistening yellow, magenta, apricot, and white of delospermas in bloom. Both cactus and ice plant flowers have a papery quality, thin, almost too thin to be real and to be so reflective — except that we have already experienced the dazzling reflectiveness like that of aluminum foil.

The woody lilies are also producers of stunning flowers, in this case magnificent in their giant spikes of many individual blooms.

Yuccas can produce spikes measured in feet, not inches, atop already tall, thick, trunklike stems with bristly balls of spearlike leaves. Even a humble rosette at ground level, itself less than a foot tall, may send up a flower stem another six feet in height.

These flowers often attract wildlife. Night-flying moths are drawn to yucca flowers, hummingbirds to those of *Hesperaloe*. I have watched families of orioles visit the towering stalks of agaves daily over the six

weeks of blossoming. As with any other plant you add to your garden, you will be creating homes or destinations for animals, too, when you put in succulents.

The chapters that follow tell a tale of my experiences and adventures with succulents in gardens in New York, Wisconsin, and Colorado. Although cold-climate gardeners can't grow the immense cactus and agaves of the desert Southwest, the gorgeous powder-blue echeverias, and all the other

tender succulents that melt when the temperature drops below freezing, they do have a wide smorgasbord of hardy succulents to sample. Often taken for granted because they are so easy to grow, here's a chance to become further acquainted with sedums and hens-and-chicks — hardy into at least USDA Zone 3. If you live in semiarid Zone 5 or 6, or more southern areas, and haven't yet tried ice plants, you are in for a treat! And if you resist the beauty of cactus and yuccas, as I once did, take another look. All these plants can be blended into modern garden designs in ways that bring new life and a novel view to the garden tapestry. Enjoy!

LEFT: *Cylindropuntia imbricata* basks in the summer light of this Delaware gravel garden.

RIGHT: *Sedum* 'Brilliant' and *Imperata cylindrica* var. *rubra* offer a blaze of red to the perennial border.

# CHAPTER I

# COMPANIONS AND STARS

Could you come to love a plant that is easy to grow, easy to weed, and easy to combine with other plants? Succulents, whether spreading mats of rounded and colorful leaves, spearlike clumps, or heavily armed guardians of the garden border, can enhance any garden design in any climate. Tumbling between stepping-stones, carpeting the soil among roses or perennials, or serving as breathtaking specimens in spectacular bloom, these actors can play minor roles or star in your garden drama. Many are eager growers, tolerant of poor soils and little water. Others thrive in dappled shade and rich soils. There are easygoing boon companions for the perennial border as well as exotic life-forms that may be grown outside in pots and provide exciting topics of conversation when friends visit your home.

Whatever your garden conditions, whatever your taste, and whatever level of energy you can devote to your landscape surroundings, I hope you will find here both new and familiar plant friends you can utilize and enjoy.

ABOVE: *Yucca flaccida* 'Golden Sword' is a bright addition to moderately moist plantings, showing beautifully here against blue spruce and the mid-green of creeping phloxes.

RIGHT: Sempervivums like the bright red and green cultivar 'Sunset' grow well in the quick-draining soils and crevices of rock gardens, or at the front of perennial beds.

## WHAT IS A SUCCULENT?

Succulents are plants that have stored water in their tissues. Thus their leaves, unlike the dry, flat leaves of trees, or even the slightly thicker leaves of vegetables like tomatoes and cabbages, are thick, turgid, and fleshy. Usually the leaves are firm, and when cut prove to be as juicy as a ripe peach. Often the leaves are rounded, as are the fat, roly-poly leaves of *Sedum divergens*, or closely ranked, as are the slender sprigs packed in along the sides of the stems of *S. acre*. In many plants the leaves are clustered low against the ground, arranged like the petals of a rose, as in the familiar hens-and-chicks (*Sempervivum*). In cactus, the stem itself is often swollen with water, the "foliage" (actually the spines) so modified as to be unrecognizable as leaves.

Succulence can be an adaptation to climates where rainfall is low, seasonal, or highly unpredictable. Many of these plants can live for months without rainfall, surviving by utilizing their stored water. Some succulents originate in moister climates, however. Sempervivums, for example, come from the high mountains of Europe; orostachys hail from moist Japan and East Asia, accustomed only to short periods of drought.

Most, but not all, hardy succulents belong to six botanical families, which are discussed on pages 18 and 19. Although there's no need to remember the technical terms by which botanists define these families, it's helpful to have some idea of their characteristics.

The fleshy, rosetted form of *Sempervivum* 'Mara' is seen in many succulents, including yuccas and agaves.

## QUESTIONS OF HARDINESS

Plant hardiness is usually understood to indicate the lowest temperature a given plant can survive. The United States Department of Agriculture (USDA) has long provided maps of the United States showing 10 zones, which are based on how low the temperature drops during the winter (see page 144). Although many plants do perish at certain low temperatures, other factors contribute to hardiness. Some plants of southwestern origin cannot survive wet winters or tolerate wet soils. Some plants require winter dormancy to thrive and bloom, and will not do well where no winter freezing occurs. Other plants can't take the "mugs" of summer in the Southeast, where both the humidity and the temperatures linger in the 90s throughout the night at midsummer.

For the purposes of this book, I consider plants that can withstand short (or long) periods of −20°F to be hardy. I live on the high Great Plains in USDA Zone 5b in Denver, Colorado, at 5,280 feet elevation, so I have tried to highlight plants that live through my winters. Many plants in this book are hardy as far north as Canada, to Zone 3, but not all are. The winter-hardy plants mentioned here are generally also good performers in Zones 6 and 7, but some drop off as the summers become hotter and more humid toward the southeastern United States, or in the hotter and almost completely dry summers of the Southwest. Others require a period of winter dormancy. There are many succulents that can be more easily grown in southern conditions than in the northern stretches of North America, and a few are mentioned within these pages. There are abundant reference texts for tender succulents, so these plants are not the focus of our attention here.

### Winter Variables

There are other factors that affect hardiness, including simply how tall a succulent is. It seems that succulents that rise more than a foot into the air above the ground become challenged during severe freezing weather. The ground is warmer than the air, the result of geothermal heat. However slight this may appear to us in winter, it seems that plants closer to the ground can survive better. Also, in winter, sap circulation within a plant is minimal, so no protection is offered by internal circulation. It isn't really surprising that succulents don't survive really cold temperatures: ice forming inside the tissues of a plant clearly do

While snow on cactus might seem out of the ordinary, many species of *Opuntia* are surprisingly hardy. Some, including this *Opuntia violacea* var. *santa-rita* (hardy to Zone 6), also take on a purplish hue in cold weather.

damage to the cell structures. Just as antifreeze in a car radiator freezes at a lower temperature than does pure water, the internal juices of succulent plants are not just water and so are able to avoid freezing below 32°F. But there are limits!

Ice plants and cactus seem to go through cold winters better if they don't receive too much water in autumn. In dry climates, reduce artificial irrigation as winter approaches. In areas with lots of autumn rainfall, consider protecting ice plants and cactus by erecting covers of glass, plastic, fiberglass, or Plexiglas. (Covers have their own challenges, wind primary among them.)

Many sedums and sempervivums need no winter protection, even in the far north.

Snow cover benefits most succulents — if only it were easy to provide! The temperature under snow is slightly warmer than in the open air, and the snow keeps the tips of agaves from "burning" (probably a result of freezing). Cactus actually seem to enjoy winter sun, and would just as soon not be covered with snow, as heavy loads of it can damage the pads of prickly pears and break the branches of chollas with just its weight. Wind damage is unusual in hardy succulents — either they are low to the ground, protected by a thick surface "skin," or they are

from dry climates and are therefore already adapted to searing breezes.

## Site Preferences

All succulents suffer if they must sit in puddles of cold water, with their roots in waterlogged soil, so be careful to plant them in well-drained soils. In climates with more than 35 inches of rainfall, especially where this rain comes in spring and autumn, succulents will often grow well in 6 to 12 inches of pure sand layered above normal soils. If you want to grow cactus that are sensitive to too much water, you may want to use a very gravelly soil. Sedums, sempervivums, and woody lilies are quite adaptable to different soils; ice plants are a bit less so, especially in moister conditions. Cactus are perhaps the most demanding if you want them to have good health, good looks, and good blossoms. (See page 137 for more information about giving cactus the proper site conditions.)

Succulents also need sun. Just as rainfall varies across the country, so do the intensity, frequency, and duration of sunlight. Generally, the more rainfall there is, the more clouds and thus the less sun. Higher elevation also increases the intensity of sun. Most hardy succulents will enjoy 8 to 12 hours of sun exposure in midsummer. A few will complain of too much heat — temperatures above 90°F during many consecutive nights, for example. In very hot, dry weather a few may grow better in partial shade. You'll have to experiment with your own site to get the best looks from your plants, as every garden has slightly different conditions, and everyone cultivates his or her garden differently. Keep in mind that south-facing slopes actually receive as much as 20 percent more solar radiation than flat ground; north-facing slopes receive proportionately less. You can use this handy fact to site plants so they receive more or less sun.

**LEFT:** Not limited to merely surviving the cold season, many succulents also offer winter interest in the garden. *Yucca faxoniana* glows in the low winter light, highlighting the dozens of curly filaments along its swordlike leaves.

**RIGHT:** Most succulents prefer well-drained soils. Rock gardens, with their gravelly soils, rock mulch, and sloping beds, offer homes to many.

# FAMILY MATTERS

EVER SINCE LINNAEUS, the famous Swedish botanist of the seventeenth century, each species of plant has had two names, a genus and a species — *Sedum spurium*, for instance. Botanists have not only assigned scientific names to each wild plant, but they have also organized plant species into related groups called plant families. These are groups of genera and species that are more closely related to each other than to other species. As in human families, these plant families share an evolutionary line and many characteristics, such as flower and seed form, some DNA and chemicals, and often some similar physiology. Learning plant families helps us to organize our knowledge of plants by comparing similar plants to each other. We also can start to generalize and predict plant behavior by family alliance: some families grow better in hot conditions, some in cool; some tolerate more severe winter temperatures.

## AGAVACEAE

Members of this family are often large plants, usually with spear- or sword-shaped leaves. They are part of a subgroup of the lily family (the Liliaceae), sometimes included in that family but always recognized as a special group. Here are the familiar yuccas and agaves, with their dramatic spikes of flowers. If you closely examine the flowers, you will find that they have six segments each, just like a lily. The leaves tend to be very fibrous and often have stringlike filaments that peel back from the margins of the leaves. Other genera coming into more common use in gardens are *Hesperaloe, Dasylirion,* and *Nolina.* Many of these plants are natives of North America.

## CRASSULACEAE

All members of this amazing family are succulents with simple, fleshy leaves. Here are found the familiar sedums and hens-and-chicks (*Sempervivum*), the spectacular rosettes of *Aeonium, Echeveria,* and *Dudleya* (though only a few species of these three genera are hardy in Zone 5), and of course the genus *Crassula*. These plants are found around the globe, except in Australia. Flowers are usually less than an inch across, with five petals, often yellow or white, but sometimes pink, scarlet, or orange. Many of these plants are very easy to propagate and some (like the ubiquitous *Sedum telephium* 'Autumn Joy') have long been stalwarts of the home garden. Yet there are many that have not been utilized as widely as they deserve.

*Agave americana,* hardy to Zone 7, is characteristic of the Agavaceae.

The Crassulaceae includes familiar plants like *Sempervivum* 'Pacific Knight'.

## MESEMBRYANTHACEAE

Members of this family are found chiefly in South Africa, where there are as many as 2,500 species! Familiar plants include the living stones (*Lithops*) and the ice plants (*Mesembryanthemum, Carpobrotus,* and their hardy counterparts in *Delosperma*). Many plants of this family, though not all, are fleshy. The flowers appear to be many-petaled (botanically speaking, the "petals" are petaloid staminodes) and most are intensely reflective, with cellular structures within the petaloids that give them a dazzling, extra-bright quality. There are usually numerous stamens, often bundled together.

In the family of the Mesembryanthaceae are the sparkly-flowered ice plants, the genus *Delosperma*.

*Echinocereus reichenbachii* has gorgeous spines elegantly arranged in flattened, radiating groups held parallel to the surface of the cactus.

## CACTACEAE

All the members of this family are succulent. Usually the leaves are so reduced as to be unrecognizable to the average person. Photosynthesis is accomplished in the stems, not in the leaves, as is more usual. The stems are swollen and may be flattened, as in the pads of the prickly pear (*Opuntia*), spherical as in ball cactus (*Pediocactus*), or cylindrical (as in the tender saguaro and in *Sclerocactus*). Flowers are often very large and multi-petaled. All but one genus are native to the New World, with some cactus in all the contiguous United States except Maine, New Hampshire, and Vermont. The reduced leaves and their bracts are transformed into spines, areoles, and glochidia. You don't need to know the technical terms, but be aware that these protective structures can be painful, toxic, and difficult to remove from your fingers — not to mention other parts of the human anatomy.

## PORTULACACEAE

This family includes plants that hail from around the world, and many, but not all, are succulent. A number of them are weeds, including that widespread annual weed purslane (*Portulaca oleracea*), which germinates so well in the first days of summer heat. The bright pink, orange, yellow, and red flowers of annual portulaca or rose moss (*Portulaca grandiflora*) are well known in horticulture, thriving in hot sun. Less common but still widely known and praised (especially in rock garden circles) are the genera *Lewisia* and *Talinum*, both native to this country. The most commonly grown, *Lewisia cotyledon*, has an evergreen rosette and pink-and-white-pin-striped flowers. All the *Talinum* species over-winter as thick, fleshy stems underground and have glossy pink, magenta, or white flowers.

The North American native *Lewisia cotyledon* has flowers as bright as its better-known cousins in the Portulacaceae.

19

# CHAPTER 2

# TINY GEMS

**ABOVE:** *Delosperma basuticum* 'Gold Nugget', a small plant to treasure, is compact and covers itself with flowers in May.

**RIGHT:** A corner of the perennial bed becomes a jewel box filled with succulents, including *Sempervivum arachnoideum, Sedum spurium* 'Tricolor', and *Sedum rupestre* 'Angelina'.

Many succulents are quite small — less than six inches tall and about as wide. Some are simply the diminutive members of several different plant families and their species — sempervivums, sedums, ice plants, cactus, and a few perennials related to portulacas, including talinums and lewisias.

These small plants can be used as ornamentation in the garden. Add interest to a close-up view of a corner by tucking a clump of hens-and-chicks at the foot of a small evergreen, in the crevice of two stones, or in a low wall. Bejewel a container or trough with one of the tiny *Sempervivum arachnoideum* selections from the Alps, each quarter-inch-wide rosette dotted in the center with bright white fuzz, all clustered together like tiny eggs in a nest, even smaller than those of hummingbirds. Or add a touch of whimsy at the top of a boulder with a small ball cactus, its spination cunning, the bright, reflective flowers an astonishing surprise in spring.

All of these offer the diverse and often charming qualities of succulence. Their bodies and leaves are plump and rounded, their colors vivid or subtle, the flowers flashy or humble. Although it is the overall habit and form of succulents that usually offers the most variety, the miniature species — nature's artwork presented for our close inspection — are as fascinating to view up close as a fine piece of tapestry, scrimshaw, or an intricate carving.

## HENS-AND-CHICKS

Hens-and-chicks are beguiling, with their plump leaves arranged in rosettes, like a double rose. Most varieties spread by producing smaller rosettes around the larger one in circles, looking like little chicks crowding around a mother hen. Sometimes these chicks are connected by runners, sometimes not.

*Sempervivum* is the genus name for these darlings, *semper* meaning forever, *vivum* meaning living. The name refers to their longevity — they seem to live forever, particularly if you think of the chicks as being the same plant as the hen. "Semps," as many gardeners call them, come in a wide variety of forms, colors, and textures. The species of hens-and-chicks are variable in nature and enthusiasts have interbred them extensively. As a result, there are more than 4,000 named varieties, differentiated by rosettes that are tighter or more open, leaves that are smooth or velvety. Some plants are covered with a doily of white spiderweb-like fibers, or the tips of their leaves are tufted with short hairs. The colors are variations on every shade of green, silver, purple, lavender, orange, red, and even yellow. And the colors usually change with the seasons, the brightest hues attained as winter shifts to spring, before the nights become too warm.

Starlike and surreal, the flowers arise on stems up to 10 inches tall, unfurling like a pin curl as they bloom along the fleshy stem. Some people like the flowers; if you don't, clip them off after a week or two. If you don't let them bloom at all, they will just keep trying. Some folks are on a quest for forms that don't flower, because after the rosette blooms, it dies, leaving a hole in the middle of the patch of chicks.

Sempervivums have close cousins in the genus *Jovibarba*. Historically, botanists have alternately lumped them in the same genus or separated them into the two genera. Jovibarbas are different in being a bit "heavier" — that is, thicker and huskier — sporting rosettes that are slightly compressed or "squished" side to side, and in having flower stems that arise from the side of the rosette rather than from the middle. I call them "jovis" for short, and I love them very much, thank you.

### Growing Semps

These plants, primarily from Europe and the European mountains, can be grown in much of the northern two-thirds of the United States and the lower part of Canada. In fact, they prefer cool nights and need a cold-dormant season to be healthy. Sempervivums thrive

in heavy, clay-based soils, but also do well in sandy soils when there is adequate moisture. Staying under four inches tall, with rosettes from half an inch to eight inches wide, they can be used at the front of a perennial border, though they perform best where they are given a bit of slope.

*In the garden.* Sempervivums can be grown between the rocks in a drystone wall or among rocks that edge a bed. Use at least three kinds and watch them mingling and tumbling, presenting a constant counter-point of interest. Such a planting changes through the seasons and over time, one variety winning more space some years, another type proving more vigorous in other years. It is also relatively carefree; sempervivums planted en masse exclude weeds fairly well. Do watch out for grasses that spread by runners, however, and keep an edge between any lawn and a bed of sempervivums. Or you could do what a lady I met in Wisconsin did: she grew her roses underplanted with an entire lawn of sempervivums. She had many varieties growing right up next to each other, completely covering the earth. Hers was a lawn that required no mowing!

**ABOVE:** Purple-tinged *Sempervivum* 'Atrovio-laceaum' takes on a sheen that makes the plant appear almost metallic.

**LEFT:** The lovely cultivar 'Zephyrine' has dark beauty and drama. Notice the crystalline white eyelash-like hairs that rim each leaf in the rosette.

# COLORFUL CHARACTERS

IT BECOMES POSSIBLE TO CLOTHE an entire garden in burgundies and greens, in whites, silvers, and reds. There are forms in which every rosette is capped with white and silver cobwebs. There are rosettes in which each leaf is tipped with a tuft of tiny hairs that stick straight up and catch the light, the dew, and the frost. In some forms the rosettes curve inward, creating rounded balls; in others, the leaves splay out wide, especially in warm weather, resembling starfish. Many forms are green toward the center of the rosette, red-tipped on the points of the leaves.

Ever sought after are the bright greens, and the urgent reds that glow in the spring with some internal fire. The red tones hold well into the warm weather, returning to dark red in autumn as temperatures drop into winter. There are outsize forms, sometimes as large as six inches across, and the tiny half-inch rollers, which tumble off as little balls whenever touched, spreading themselves to new locations. There are silvers, sometimes with lavender over- or undertones; there are pale pinks, oranges, mysterious cheesy tones of yellow-green; there are strange murky grays, leaves as dark as midnight and velvety rosettes with short hairs across the surface of the leaf; there are crisp jovibarbas with sharp-tipped leaves crowded upon each other. The hens-and-chicks provide much to love and admire.

*SEMPERVIVUM 'FARAMIR'*

*SEMPERVIVUM ZELLEBORI*

SEMPERVIVUM 'GOLD BUG'

SEMPERVIVUM 'GLOWING EMBERS'

SEMPERVIVUM CALCAREUM

SEMPERVIVUM MARMOREUM

SEMPERVIVUM 'MONASES'

JOVIBARBA HIRTA

In a rock garden, sempervivums can fill narrow spots between rocks, keeping the soil in place, providing a foil for larger plants, and complementing other small plants. They look great at the foot of slightly taller plants, serving as a living mulch. When planted together, they can create a low pool or stream across the floor of rock garden valleys.

*In containers.* Hens-and-chicks grow superbly in pots, both by themselves and with other plants. You can use just one kind and watch the chicks drape themselves over the edge of the pot and down to the ground. If you use two kinds, choose those that look good together but also *different* from each other — in color, texture, size, or hairiness.

For height and textural variety, add an interesting rock to your pot. Or put in three, and over time the sempervivums will knit the rocks together. Sometimes I use a large pot and rocks arranged like an outcrop, and plant as many as 10 kinds of semps.

Did I mention that these plants are easy to grow? They are *very* easy to grow and satisfyingly simple to propagate —just pull off a chick and stick its stem in the ground. They can be killed by intense drought, by soggy site conditions, and by being overgrown or shaded out by taller plants. Of course, nothing *really* lives forever, but certainly these are long-lived plants. I suppose they live on and on in successive generations of geneti-

A variety of sempervivums grown in a trough or pot makes a pretty picture and brings these small plants up higher where you can see them without kneeling.

## CONTAINER COMPANIONS

The possibilities for growing small succulents in containers are almost endless. In addition to stunning structure and gorgeous foliage, no container will be easier to maintain through the year. Sedums and sempervivums are good partners, because they have approximately the same growing requirements: good sandy or clay loam, a soil just heavy enough to hold them in place (*not* soilless, peat-based mix), and a moderate supply of water. Some suggestions for combinations are:

**Green and red.** The green, toothed foliage of *Sedum* 'Weihenstephaner Gold' with a dark maroon sempervivum like 'Rex' or 'Dark Point' and a bright red sempervivum like 'Madame Arsac' or the adorable and smaller 'Jewel Box'.

**Copper and lime.** The rounded leaves of *Sedum ewersii* 'Rosenteppich' with a coppery form of *Orostachys iwarenge* and a lime green form of the petite *Orostachys spinosa* 'Minutissima' (for a shady spot).

**Silver and pink.** The low and eversilvery blue-green *Sedum pachyclados* might overwhelm the smaller sempervivums, but would combine very well with those with larger rosettes, such as 'Commander Hay' or 'Plum Pink'. For a hotter look, try it with *Jovibarba* 'Hot Lips' or 'Sylvan Memory'.

cally identical chicks, probably living longer than we do. Which is a comforting thought. They're also remarkably hardy; all the sempervivums are hardy at least to Zone 3.

### Plant Selection

Described below are a few of the most common species — also the most commonly used in hybrids. Because of the thousands of hybrids between the species, most hens-and-chicks are identified primarily by their cultivar names. (Cultivar names are enclosed by single quotes; they are not the same as common names, although they are usually in English. Common names, confusingly, can apply to an entire genus, to different species, or even to plants that are totally unrelated to each other.) Don't bother trying to trace the heritage of a given named cultivar; it may be impossible. It's difficult enough to keep the names on all the cultivars — believe me, I know! And once the names become separated from the plants, please don't give them new names. It only confuses an already confusing situation, as if stepchildren had one name at one house and another at the other parent's. Just enjoy them!

### ❋ Sempervivum arachnoideum

A distinctive species, this has long hairs joining the leaf tips, forming a perfect white spider web in each rosette (hence the species name *arachnoideum*). They hail from

A single selection of *Sempervivum arachnoideum* spills down the face of a rock. Somehow this plant produces spiderweb–like hairs that stretch as the rosettes grow wider.

the southern slopes of the Alps, which are well watered, so don't expect it to thrive in really dry conditions in hot climates. However, excellent drainage is also necessary! Flowers are usually a lovely, chalky pink. Some favorite cultivars with *S. arachnoideum* heritage include 'Kammerer's Spinnrad', 'Downland Queen', and 'Rubrum'.

### ❋ *Sempervivum ciliosum*

This species is native to the Balkans. Hairs at the leaf edges of these plants form silvery eyelashes; flowers are soft yellow. There are many cultivars with heavily tipped leaves, which are probably derived from this species. They are intensely charming to gaze down at, especially when backlit in the early spring.

### ❋ *Sempervivum calcareum*

Although it usually occurs on limey (or calcareous, hence its name) substrates in nature, it does not seem fussy about conditions in the garden. Rosettes of blue-green are tipped with vivid mahogany. Some favorite cultivars are 'Mrs. Giuseppe', the enchanting 'Pink Pearl', and 'Sir William Lawrence'.

### ❋ *Jovibarba heuffelii*

Regarded by many as the king of the hen-and-chicks, this extremely variable species, also from the Balkans, is placed in another genus. Rather than producing "chicks," the rosettes split in two down the middle, giving it a side-to-side compressed look. The blooming rosettes produce their flowering stems from the side rather than from the center. A number of cultivars have been bred, many with brilliant contrasts of green and mahogany, resulting in such dramatic names as 'Hot Lips', 'Brocade', 'Sylvan Memory', and 'Gold Bug'.

### ❋ *Jovibarba arenaria, J. hirta,
J. allionii,* and *J. sobolifera*

These four rather small species originate in southern Europe. The smooth, bright green leaves make very tight, rounded plants that are positively ball-like in some forms. The "chicks" usually emerge from the middle leaves, like small round marbles, and roll off the mother plant at the slightest nudge to form new plants nearby.

LEFT: *Sempervivum calcareum* 'Sir William Lawrence' shows the typical dark red leaf tips of the species.

RIGHT: The jovibarbas are huskier and heavier than sempervivums and show a slight lateral compression of the rosette, visible here in *Jovibarba* 'Fanfare'.

## DIMINUTIVE SEDUMS

Sedums are a varied tribe with more than 300 species around the world. Happily, many are quite small, less than a foot in height and often less than six inches across, and so they are appropriate for small niches in the garden. They are loosely rooted plants (as opposed to taprooted or deeply rooted). Their plump little leaves may be smooth-edged or cunningly toothed. Some bear bright yellow flowers, some white, a few pink, but the flowers are not their main attraction. The evergreen leaves — sometimes ever red, ever maroon, ever blue-gray, or ever silvery blue — offer interest at all times of year, whenever there is no snow cover.

### Growing Sedums

The sedums are largely plants of the Northern Hemisphere, and they do most of their growing in the cool weather of spring and fall. Climates with cool nights (where the temperature drops below 70°F) delight them, although sedums as a group are among the most tolerant of garden plants. Some sedums require really good drainage, especially those that are native to mountains; some, such as those hailing from the coasts of Oregon and Washington state, need a bit more moisture and possibly shade in very sunny climates.

In general, the smaller the plant, the more one needs to protect it from garden hazards such as aggressive companions, rambunctious dogs, and reckless visitors. Small plants can easily be destroyed by small accidents. Because the sedums are not highly centralized around a single rootstock, it is generally simple to divide them. Also, the stems root easily, so propagating them from cuttings is a cinch.

### Plant Selection

I've chosen the following selections because they are widely available and because they are especially charming. Like sempervivums, they'll make you want to start a collection.

### ✿ Sedum ewersii var. homophyllum 'Rosy Carpet'

This sedum forms a beautiful, mounded mat of rounded blue-green leaves, topped by rosy flowers held just above the foliage. The mat, usually dense, opens up in too much shade. It's delightful with fall gentians and oreganos or all by itself. 'Rosy Carpet' needs part shade (or the north side of a rock) in sunny climates or at high elevation. There are other forms of this species, but this is my favorite.

LEFT: The heavily toothed, closely packed rosettes of *Sedum pachyclados* are enchanting in a rock garden or at the front of a border. In either situation, give it a bit of shade.

### ✽ *Sedum spathulifolium* 'Cape Blanco'

This small, broochlike jewel is perfect for adorning the low crevices of a rock garden or the edge of a woodland path. It is native to shady cliffs in Oregon, within the sound of the sea. Beautifully glaucous, almost white leaves form loose rosettes highlighted with touches of green and red. To see it is to desire it. Being no fan of muggy, hot weather, this plant delights in coolth. Place it where it has afternoon shade, at least, and where it will be neither too wet nor too dry. This one may be challenging to grow, but it's worth trying many times until you find a permanent home for it in your garden. Another selection worth considering is 'Harvest Moon'.

### ✽ *Sedum makinoi* 'Ogon'

A recent yellow-foliaged introduction, this sedum will brighten parts of the garden in dappled shade. It holds its flat round leaves parallel to the ground, as much as 4 inches high, spreading to about 10 inches in a year. Plant in sun in moist climates; shade or part shade is better in hot, sunny areas. Although it is somewhat drought-tolerant, it wants some moisture to grow well and look happy. It's especially lovely when paired with variegated foliage, such as that of miniature hostas, *Brunnera* 'Jack Frost', Japanese painted fern (*Athyrium nipponicum* 'Pictum'), *Heuchera* 'Snow Angel', or *Polemonium* 'Brise d'Anjou'. It makes an equally beautiful contrast with the dark green leaves of cyclamen and gingers, or the bronze tones of the many dark-leaved coralbells. Pair it with the pale blue flowers of dwarf iris or Jacob's ladder in spring, with gentians in a semi-shaded rock garden, or with the bright pink flowers of coralbells in early summer.

**TOP LEFT:** Hailing from the Oregon coast, *Sedum* 'Cape Blanco' is so glaucous that one could imagine it being dewy from the sea mist.

**TOP RIGHT:** The golden leaves of *Sedum* 'Ogon' brighten the shady garden. It seems to be very weakly rooted, so handle with care!

## OROSTACHYS

The dim shadows of a woodland or rock garden can be brightened and cheered by a group of plants from the Far East, the genus *Orostachys*. A varied tribe related to both sedums and sempervivums (but less well known), specimens form tiny mats of rosettes and in very late fall produce the most surprising inverted cones of flowers, which look like elongated dunce caps or narrow towers of tiny blooms. The inflorescence is a spike, both exotic and suggestive, and may cause a stir at late-summer garden parties.

Although there are only a dozen or fewer species, they are so fancifully colored, so otherworldly that you may want to grow them all. Hailing from Japan and northern Asia, they like well-shaded areas, although they may also grow in full sun — even in Colorado — where water is sufficient and plant companions cool their roots. *Orostachys aggregata* has bright green leaves; *O. fimbriata* is a steely, moody blue-gray; *O. furusei* (*O. boehrmeri*) has gray, lavender, and brown overtones or can even boast bright greens.

My heart's desire is the more difficult to find and keep *O. erubescens,* a glowing, succulent green suffused and edged with emberlike red. *Orostachys chanettii* has done well in part shade, looking lovely in the company of *Delosperma dyeri,* the bright flowers of the ice plant picking up the red tones of the orostachys rosette.

You might want to plant these tiny strangers in the shade of a dwarf conifer, where they can intertwine with a mat-forming veronica. Orostachys also look wonderful alongside a staircase, where you can see them at eye level as you ascend. Planted atop a wall in the rock garden, the little pagodas will grab your attention in late summer, as the rest of the garden fades into its autumn rest. These plants are also well placed at the base of a large tree, where the boll of the tree gives them an uncluttered background for their petite yet striking display.

There is a very tightly rosetted species, *Orostachys spinosa,* whose every leaf is tipped with a spine. It enjoys more sun than the others, at home with a full southern exposure. It also does well in dry conditions. Grow it amid a tumult of creeping veronica or atop a flat rock, in a crevice, or in containers.

Orostachys definitely need shade or part shade in dry, sunny climates and don't want to dry out. In my garden, they live through some winters and die out in others. This is partly because the rosettes that bloom die, and sometimes they all bloom. With the exception of *O. spinosa* (hardy to Zone 4), they aren't likely to survive much north of Zone 5b and probably not south of Zone 8, especially if it is dry as well as hot, or if it is extremely hot at night. These plants evolved in a climate like that of Japan — cool and moist and tempered by the ocean — and would be quite happy in coastal Oregon and Washington.

**OPPOSITE LEFT AND RIGHT:** Here you can see two different moods of the same species, *Orostachys spinosa.* The plant on the left is grown with less light and more water than the one on the right.

**RIGHT:** The gentle, petite rosettes of *Orostachys furusei* are humble and subtle enough until August begins to wane. Then the flower spikes, seen here, shoot up like a small gathering of gnomes.

## BALL AND BARREL CACTUS

The ball cactus are a very special group of plants, not like any others on the planet. They vary from the commonly known prickly pears in that they are compact and don't have leaves or branches or pads — just balls or upright cylindrical barrels. Most have dense spination that surrounds the plant body, but not long spines that stick out away from the plant and catch passersby unawares. That is, they are easier to be around and easier to handle, as they can often be picked up and planted with bare hands, without any spines remaining in the hands of the gardener. Ball and barrel cactus may look much alike to the beginner, although there are differences in how the spines are arranged; if you want to get technical or if you have the perceptions of a structural engineer, perhaps these will be obvious to you.

**ABOVE:** With age, *Echinocereus reichenbachii* var. *caespitosus* forms pups (a small one is seen at center). As each pup elongates into adulthood, a cluster of cylinders forms, striking at all times of year.

**RIGHT:** *Echinocereus reichenbachii* var. *baileyi*; keeps company with *Delosperma basuticum* and a cultivar of *Sempervivum arachnoideum*.

These plants not only are remarkable in their structure and design, but they also bear lovely, wide-open, pearlescent flowers that shine reflectively in the sun. The flowers range from scarlet to orange to pink to pale yellow to lime green.

### Growing Ball and Barrel Cactus
All cactus are susceptible to rot and fungal disease when grown in wet climates (those with more than 30 inches of rain annually, especially where that rain is evenly distributed through the calendar year). In semiarid regions like the western Great Plains, the desert Southwest, and the Intermountain West, you can grow cactus in well-drained, unwatered clay soils. Don't try this in the East! If you have more than 30 inches of annual rainfall and live north of the Mason-Dixon line, plant cactus in gravelly soil or pure sand up to 18 inches deep. Choose a south-facing exposure or, even better, a south-facing *slope*, or grow your treasures in containers in a specially prepared soil mix, with as much as half gravel or scoria (volcanic gravel).

### Plant Selection
When you buy them, ball and barrel cactus will usually be small plants, a single ball or cylinder, or a small clump of succulent balls. Over the years they'll become larger clumps, some as big as six inches across. If you succeed in growing a large clump, gradually move plants away from the cactus, as too much crowding or shading will have a negative impact on this sun-loving plant. The clumps form because the cylinders or balls produce small "pups" on one side, and these then grow into larger cylinders or balls. These darling plants make points of interest in troughs, small cactus gardens, and among native grasses, as *Coryphantha vivipara* does on the wild wide prairies of Wyoming.

### ✳ *Pediocactus simpsonii*

As a baby, this plant is perhaps an inch across, a very round ball. My favorite forms have bright white spines so dense that they look like snowballs. As they grow, the balls get wider and a bit taller, reaching at least six inches across and three inches in height. They may also pup, forming small replicas of themselves around the oldest ball.

The flowers are usually pink, often large and breathtaking. Other forms have pale yellow blossoms. All bloom in very early April. These lovely, surprising plants were once abundant on the plains at the feet of the Rocky Mountains; now suburbs have replaced them by the thousands. This plant will not tolerate overwatering, so if you grow it where cold rains fall in autumn and spring, protect it under glass, Plexiglas, or the wide eaves of a building. Zone 2 and south.

### ✳ *Echinocereus reichenbachii*

A lanky-cowboy barrel, widespread in the American Southwest, this little cactus is taller than it is wide. The tallest are about 10 inches. It may have spines of white, black, pale yellow, or even red. The flowers are usually shining magenta, sometimes pale straw-yellow. A number of subspecies are quite hardy when they're given good sun and drainage. It is happy to grow in the shelter of a west- or south-facing rock on a scree or

Closely packed red and white spines look gorgeous when backlit here in *Echinocereus viridiflorus*. This plant is taller than other specimens of this species: it's a Texan.

in a rock garden. There are many selections available — try several from different areas of the West. Zone 5 and south.

Plant this species with a low-growing dryland plant such as black-eye daisy (*Leucanthus melanocephalus*) or *Zinnia grandiflora*, but protect it from being overgrown by taller plants. It also looks good and prospers in the shade of a dryland shrub — though you may need to prune the shrub away from it every year or two. Penstemons are good companions; becausee they are low rosettes through much of the year, the cactus receives its share of sun.

*Echinocereus viridiflorus* is smaller — a low, rounded ball, greenish and unobtrusive, with lime green flowers produced early in spring. Combine it with a bright orange cowboy's delight (*Spharalcea coccinea*) or Indian paintbrush (*Castilleja* sp.) — have a little fun! Zone 3 and south.

### ✳ *Echinocereus triglochidiatus*

This is a variable species that grows across Utah, Texas, and Arizona. The cylinders may be only an inch tall in the variety *coccineus* or more than a foot tall in southern forms. The flowers are brilliant red-orange and chalice-shaped and, interestingly, don't vary much. In nature these plants seem to prefer rock crevices, although in the garden they may be grown on a slope of gravelly soil or even on flat ground, if your climate is very dry. It is quite a surprise and delight to come across a "trig" (as they're sometimes called) in the desert — very old plants may have 200 cylinders huddled together in a clump three feet across. Sure, the clump itself has merely a sort of gray-green appearance, like a lumpy beach ball that's as solid as a rock. But what about the hundreds of brilliant carmine flowers? These are massive plants that, in their maturity, deserve the respect due to elders; they bring great substance, solemnity, and dignity to the garden.

The cultivar 'Giant Texan' has very, very tall cylinders, up to a foot. The flowers are true orange, whereas those of most other "triglochs" are red-orange flowers. The longer and taller the cylinders, the more likely the plant is to be "bitten" by the harsh and icy daggers of sudden deep frost. Protect it north of Zone 6, either by warm microclimate, rock crevice, or deep snow, or by planting it in a pot and bringing it onto a cool porch for the winter.

The variety *coccineus*, in its many incarnations, is a shortened version of *Echinocereus triglochidiatus* with dense golden spines. It's hardier — witness its northerly range — probably because it's a small plant that stays low to the ground. Zone 5 and south.

### ✳ *Escobaria orcuttii*

This is one of my favorite small cactus, because it is such a perfect white ball. It has grown for 10 years now in a trough outside my garden in Denver, unprotected winter and summer. It is two to three inches across, with white spines — like a desert snowball.

Its Texas cousin *Escobaria echinus* is also quite small and has pastel yellow flowers; it is probably not quite as hardy, but does well in my Zone 5 garden. Both of these should be grown in containers or with other small plants in a dry garden. Zone 5 and south.

### ✳ *Escobaria vivipara*

This can form quite a large ball, perhaps six to eight inches across, surrounded by its own starlike spines, the branches held flat and parallel to the surface of the ball. It may bear as many as a dozen gleaming, rosy pink flowers in May, June, or July, depending on how northerly your zone is. It is native as far north as Alberta and southwest Manitoba. Dazzling varieties occur farther south, from the Mojave Desert to the big bend of Texas. As your specimen matures, it will only become more beautiful.

## CACTUS: A WORD ABOUT PLURALS

The word *cactus* is derived from the Greek *kaktos*, and has been used in botanical Latin since Linnaeus's time. Its formal plural in Latin is *cacti*, but since it has become part of the English language, it's been given the plural *cactuses*. Some people also use *cactus* as a plural, as in "one cactus, two cactus," giving it sort of a mass noun status, like sheep: one sheep, two sheep. There are arguments to be made for any of the three usages, but in this book we use the last choice, whether referring to a single cactus or many.

Use *Escobaria* species in containers; in very well drained, gravelly beds; or in a hot, sloping xeric garden near a path, where it can be appreciated. Small penstemons, such as *Penstemon eriantherus* and *P. virens*, or some of the low eriogonums, such as *Eriogonum kennedyi*, *E. jamesii*, and *E. caespitosum*, will enjoy its company. Dryland hymenoxys, *Veronica liwanensis*, cowboy's delight (*Spharalcea coccinea*), partridge feather (*Tanacetum densum* var. *amanum*), *Zinnia grandiflora*, and any other truly xeric, small perennials would be equally good companion plants. Zone 3 and south.

### ✽ *Escobaria sneedii* subsp. *sneedii*

A very tiny cactus and an endangered species from near Carlsbad Caverns, in south-ern New Mexico, this cactus should be purchased only from a reputable grower who doesn't collect plants from the wild. It seems to do quite well in cultivation. The balls of this cactus are very white and tiny, the largest perhaps three and a half inches across; the small offsets are marble-size or even smaller. As the plants age, they pup liberally, surrounding themselves with many smaller offspring. The flowers are thin in texture, shiny, and pale pink.

This is a plant for the trough or container garden, or for a prominent niche in the garden, in full sun. By planting it in a container, though, you bring it into closer focus, making it easier to see and admire. It grows well with other ball cactus, with the smallest of the dryland penstemons, with petite plants such as *Lesquerella alpina*, *Phlox hoodii*, or *Townsendia exscapa*. In moist climates, protect the entire container from the cold rains of spring and fall, and place it where it has good air circulation. Should you plant it in the garden, provide perfect drainage. Zone 5 and south.

ABOVE: *Escobaria sneedii* subsp. *sneedii* is a perfect plant for display in its own pot or in a dryland trough. Although endangered in nature, it is easily cultivated when obtained from permitted sources.

LEFT: *Escobaria* (formerly *Coryphantha*) *missouriensis* has gorgeous, straw-colored flowers. Note the dark green, plumped up body below the spines, indicating that this plant is grown in a climate with extra water and a bit of shade.

## TINY ICE PLANTS

Ice plants are members of the tropical family Aizoaceae and hail from South Africa. Although one might think of South Africa as a tropical country, apparently many plants, especially in the Draakensberg Mountains, have retained what could be termed "residual hardiness" from the long years before the continents drifted apart, when Africa was farther north. Thus we find some plants with a surprising ability to survive at least as far north as Zone 5 if they are protected from excessive moisture.

### Growing Ice Plants

Ice plants have a high quantity of internal water, and all that water makes the plants susceptible to rot from the outside. Grow ice plants in rock garden soils (generally that means with at least one part quarter-inch gravel and nearly two parts sharp sand, which has particles that don't pack tightly together) with two parts loam and one part humus.

Many of these ice plants appreciate having their crowns between two rocks or at least up against a rock on one side; this allows water to drain promptly from their thick, central roots. The demand for rapid drainage does not, however, mean that the

**LEFT:** *Delosperma basuticum* 'White Nugget' snuggles here between two rocks. It is more of a clump-former than a ground cover, always maintaining closely packed foliage and spreading slowly. It covers itself with flowers in May.

**RIGHT:** Here is a dwarf form of *Delosperma congestum,* the flowers smaller than those of 'Gold Nugget'. The foliage turns a lovely merlot color in winter.

## PLANTING WITH ROCKS

Rocks are often added to a garden to bring a bit of variety and topography to the design, or because rocks are beautiful and interesting in their own right. However, they can also benefit the plants in the garden. When sunk a few inches or more into the soil, a rock adds to the rapid drainage of the soil near it. It can provide a bit of shade on the north side. Because rocks are so dense, they change temperature more slowly than the soil near them, providing extra warmth in spring and fall and extra hours of cool temperatures in summer. Some plants simply seem to enjoy growing in rocky soil or between two rocks or just near a rock. There they look larger than life and well-grounded in the garden scene.

plants don't need water at all. They still have to drink; they just don't want to sit in soggy soil. In climates where cold rain falls on frozen soil, give them especially sharp drainage and an inch of gravel mulch. Decrease watering as autumn deepens, to induce dormancy before a hard freeze. All prefer full sun and appreciate a south-facing slope.

### Plant Selection

Discussed below are some of the smaller plants of this family, not really ground covers but plants that form tight clumps. Use them to brighten small niches in a rock garden or in a raised bed with dryland plants on a small scale. They will also thrive in unmortared garden walls on steep, south-facing slopes.

### ❋ Delosperma sphalmanthoides

This is truly a gem of the plant world, with tiny, blue-green, fingerlike leaves held upward in a small disk that may grow to three or four inches in diameter. In early spring, these leaves will suddenly be topped with wide, shining magenta flowers. This plant seems to do best in the company of rocks, where it has a cool root run. In fact, growing with rocks slows the heating and cooling of the soil and provides sharp drainage and additional water at the same time. I have most often grown this plant in a crevice within my rock garden. However, it will also do well in a trough or container. Zones 5 to 9.

### ❋ Delosperma 'Gold Nugget'

This is thought to be a sport of the more common *Delosperma basuticum* (the fertile version of the very similar *D. nubigenum*). It forms a very tight mound of fat, light green, leaves and looks great among rocks. It has many, many bright, shiny yellow flowers. The similar 'White Nugget' bears white flowers, and its winter foliage seems to be a more gray green. Zones 4 to 8.

# OTHER PETITE PLANTS

The following are assorted small plants, not always readily available in commerce, but still delightful. They come from families with fewer well-known small members and are included here for gardeners looking for petite players in the garden drama.

### ❀ *Aloinopsis* spp.

Plants in this genus form clumps of thick, succulent leaves; the leaves are all close upon the ground and the flowers are borne on the foliage, such that there are no obvious stems. They produce spectacular flowers, covering the foliage in bright yellows to reds to magentas and every shade in between. The rosettes of leaves sit atop large, carrotlike roots that must be protected from excessive moisture.

*Aloinopsis spathulata* is a small, jewellike plant, with tight mounds of spathulate (almost spoon-shaped), succulent, wavy blue-green leaves. In spring, the foliage is obscured by the large, sparkling magenta flowers.

There are now many hybrids between *Aloinopsis* and *Nananthus* species that may be more reliably winter-hardy than either parent. A number of wonderful selections are being produced by Sunscapes, a rare-plant nursery in Pueblo, Colorado. Zone 5 and south.

*Lewisia tweedyi* hails from the mountains east of Seattle, blooming in a few places in abundance under the light shade of pines. This plant prefers a site in a rock garden with part-shade and the company of rocks.

### *Lewisia cotyledon*

This is a famous and much-loved plant among rock gardeners. It comes from a genus named after Meriwether Lewis, of the Lewis and Clark expedition, which brought so many western plants to the attention of the white settlers and Europeans for the first time. The leaves are thick and usually dark green, sometimes toothed, and arranged in rosettes close to the ground. The flowers in the wild forms are candy-striped pink and white, bright and cheerful when they appear in midspring. Cultivated varieties may have dark pink, bright orange, shiny white, purplish pink, and even golden flowers.

Native to the Pacific Northwest, lewisias have become favorites of many gardeners, especially in Europe. In nature they bloom and grow in the dappled shade of pines, in rocky, mineral soils. You can grow them in rock gardens, where they have a sloping, loose, sandy or clay-loam soil that never stays too damp. They enjoy the company of rocks and grow well in crevices — try them among rocks in a pot.

I can never have enough lewisias! They grow easily from seed, so I try to have at least a dozen in my garden at any time, and add more every year. For most people, lewisias don't live much more than five years, although this is likely because we aren't providing exactly what they want, rather than because they aren't long-lived. Zones 3 to 8.

### *Stomatium mustillinum*

This plant forms tight clumps of closely held gray-green, curving leaves, scoop-shaped and roughened with many minute white dots. Inch-wide, shining yellow flowers spread their abundant narrow petals in late-afternoon sunshine, beckoning bees. The flowers close to a pointed cone-shaped bud at night and in cloudy weather. This specimen is a must for those who admire weird

## IN THE COLLECTOR'S GARDEN

The following plants are a bit more difficult to find in the trade. All of them need some special care; they are for the dedicated gardener willing to grow them in containers, in a rock garden, or a specially prepared bed.

**Dudleya cymosa** A member of the Crassulaceae, *Dudleya cymosa* seems to be the hardiest of the tribe of dudleyas and escobarias, so lovely in frost-free climates — and so mushy in the North. *Dudleya cymosa* has gorgeous, turgid, glaucous blue rosettes about five inches across. This plant probably requires a tight, south-facing crevice between two rocks. Bright orange flowers are produced on a short scape in late spring or midsummer. This dudleya is hardy most years in Denver, (Zone 5) but it doesn't seem to live many

years. In Pueblo, Colorado, 100 miles south, it is much more reliable. The beauty of the plant makes it worth replacing a few times, but it is not for the timid.

**Othonna capensis** This is an amusing little plant in the sunflower family. It forms loose mats of chubby, cylindrical, blue-green leaves, which have earned it the common name "little pickles." Tiny, bright yellow, daisylike flowers appear on wiry, two-inch-high stems held just above the mats. It has a long season of bloom. We don't know yet just what it wants to be durably happy: for some gardeners it persists as long as five years; however, for many others, this plant is as fleeting as a good joke. It's a must for the succulent fancier, no matter how long it lasts. Hardy to Zone 5.

**DUDLEYA CYMOSA**

plant forms. The stomatiums are admired not for their symmetry, as the sempervivums are, but rather for their unique, unfamiliar leaf texture and the overall aspect of something from a distant land — or planet!

*Stomatium agninum* has dull-green, roughened, green-dotted leaves, very attractive in its unusual character. Flowers are pale yellow, although the plant appears too shy to bloom often, at least in my Colorado garden. *Stomatium beaufortense* has mid-green foliage with small white dots and a few short teeth along the margins; flowers are yellow. *Stomatium loganii* is a similar cousin. Zone 5 and south.

### ❋ *Talinum* spp.

Members of this genus in the portulaca family also provide entertainment for the succulent lover. All have plump, cylindrical leaves growing from a thick stem or root stalk. All are excellent plants for commuter-gardeners, as the flowers open in late afternoon, just as workers are returning home. All thrive in poor sandy soil or dry loose clay in full sun. Most are hardy as far north as Zone 3 and as far south as the Mexican border. They are warm-weather growers and don't mind the heat one bit. Most also tolerate humidity.

*Talinum calycinum* is perhaps the best-known species, rising from a thick stem to a tuft of multidirectional leaves, spreading out like plump pick-up-sticks about four inches in all directions. Then comes a burst of bright, shiny, metallic pink flowers on almost invisible wirelike stems. These plants are delightful — partly, I think, because they are so surprising. They surprise again, if they like your conditions, by self-sowing and appearing in new places each year. *Talinum spinescens* is a smaller version of *T. calycinum*, forming more-condensed mounds with the same hot magenta flowers. *Talinum rugospermum* is a species from sandy and rocky prairies atop bluffs in the plains of the Midwest. It will do very well in almost pure sand or on rocky ledges.

*Talinum brevifolium* is a tiny thing that would likely be lost in the garden — an ironic fact, as it grows in a vast uninhabited region of Utah called the San Rafael Swell, which has no human residents for 100 square miles and where outlaws lost themselves from the attentions of the law. However, *T. brevifolium* is an excellent denizen of troughs and a boon companion for cactus and other small dryland species that need protection from the overexuberance of more-common garden perennials. The sausage-shaped, opalescent leaves, mostly laid flat upon the ground, bear many cheerful pink, half-inch flowers on summer evenings. *Talinum brachypodium* is similar. *Talinum sedoides* is even tinier, with tufts of as many as a dozen, eighth-inch-long leaves and half-inch pink flowers; use it with small ball cactus as a ground cover in the miniature landscape of a trough.

All the talinums present a challenge to the gardener's memory: they are deciduous and disappear after frost, except for the succulent rootstock. If you weed over them, you may pull them out and destroy them, so note carefully where your patches are. Protect them from your own urges to clean up in spring and fall. Most species should be hardy to Zone 4 and south.

### ❋ *Yucca harrimaniae*

One of just a few small, hardy yuccas, *Y. harrimaniae* features many curly filaments within the rosettes, which make this species particularly fetching. The species is extremely variable, with many selections that are quite small, some to only 10 inches in rosette or even smaller in "dollhouse" forms. These are the smallest of the yuccas, a great species for a small-scale garden and places where space is at a premium. Some forms pup quite prolifically, forming wide colonies of quaint dwarfs. *Yucca nana* is one of several selections and is also quite small. Zones 4 to 8.

*Yucca nana,* sometimes grouped with *Yucca harrimaniae,* seems the smallest of the outdoor yuccas; a young plant may be only six inches across. They also pup, forming solid clumps of rosettes.

# CHAPTER 3

# CONTAINERS

**ABOVE:** *Sempervivum* 'Sugaree' is one of some 4,000 cultivars of this charming genus. All semps are easy to grow in pots.

**RIGHT:** This urn is full of frost-tender succulents — echeverias of three types and a burro's-tail sedum — cavorting with a pair of hardy hens-and-chicks and the vining *Dichondra argentea*.

Succulents are excellent candidates for containers, because they don't require large amounts of water. A pot of succulents may require less than half the water a pot of tropical plants or annuals needs. Containers of colorful and symmetrical sempervivums, toothed or chubby-leaved sedums, or bristly cactus can add novel textures and colors to a grouping of many containers that include flowering annuals as well. And because succulents are grown for their showy, plump bodies as much as for their flowers, they provide a longer-lasting display than many traditional container plantings do, usually looking nice throughout the year.

Think of a pot as a small garden in a frame. You can create a miniature landscape by adding a rock or two. You can add a small conifer for height or interest. The pot frames the picture and isolates this small garden from the rest of your landscape.

If succulents are good for pots, pots are likewise excellent for the culture of succulents, as they can provide perfect drainage for these plants, which so often require it. The pots also isolate smaller succulents from the perils of the open garden (more-aggressive plants and marauding animals that might trample them). Planting in pots enables you to use fast-draining soil mixes, especially important for cactus, which must have excellent drainage.

## SOILS FOR POTS

The first item to decide when potting a succulent is the soil composition. For sedums and sempervivums, compose a potting mix of about half or even two-thirds "good garden soil." Either a clay- or sand-based loam will do equally well. Garden soil is a wonderful and somewhat mysterious material with a range of particle sizes. It almost always has a bit of clay, which provides nutrients and has the ability to slowly release both nutrients and water. Add a bit of organic matter, such as leaf mold or coarse peat moss, a dash of well-rotted manure, and perhaps some ⅛-inch to ⅜-inch gravel to keep the soil open, so that oxygen can reach the roots.

I avoid using prepared potting soil that contains considerable perlite, because the little white beads float when the soils are heavily watered. I don't like the look of all those "pearls" at the top of the soil, and I also think that this lightweight material makes the plants more subject to frost heaving in times when the soils are freezing and thawing during cold weather. The freezing of soil water pushes around the plant roots and tends to lift the plants out of the soil.

Vermiculite, also used in some commercial potting soils, is less conspicuous than perlite because it is darker in color, and it doesn't float as easily. Nevertheless, be care-

**LEFT:** *Carnegia gigantea* basks in the low sunlight of a summer evening. It's especially at home in a pot, where it can be given the fast-draining soil it needs to thrive and taken in for the winter.

**RIGHT:** *Agave weberi* 'Arizona Star' (center) and *Agave desmettiana* 'Joe Hoak' (right) add drama to the summer patio. However, they are only summer guests in the North, hardy to about Zone 8.

ful not to use more than about a fifth of this material in your potting soil.

A third lightweight soil additive is popped or baked clay, available in several brands, depending on your location. This material often looks like kitty litter. It has been processed to high temperatures so that it doesn't break down when watered. Unlike soil clay, it doesn't pack together, but instead maintains itself as distinct particles, keeping the soil loose while still providing the nutrient- and water-holding properties of clay.

It's clear that cactus shouldn't be grown in waterlogged soils, where the roots and even the base of the plant body may rot. Don't use more than about a third garden soil for these plants in containers. The goal is to compose an *open* soil — one with lots of oxygen within the soil and room for water to drain through rapidly — with lots of mineral components, like grit, gravel, and scoria, which do not hold much water and do not compact. Do not include heavy doses of organic materials like leaf mold and peat moss, which hold quite a bit of water and may bring in organisms that lead to rot. Take care not to make your soil too high in sand, which can also hold an amazing amount of water, especially in humid or rainy weather. Although most of the water drains through sand quickly, the ability of sand to wick water upward is greater than you might think, as its particle size actually attracts water.

### Soil Temperatures

Because of its sheer lack of mass, the soil in a container heats up more rapidly than does the open soil of a garden. Both the soil

and the pot heat up most in the intense sun of a southern exposure, and this may have a beneficial effect on controlling fungi and other soilborne diseases that will compromise the health especially of desert succulents like cactus and agaves.

My succulent pots are unprotected by cover in winter; the cactus are placed on the south-facing side of a large blue spruce, where the pots are warmed by sun and protected from north winds. The containers of sempervivums and sedums usually just stay where they are, even raised on the low stone wall of the vegetable garden. Sometimes I set the pots on the ground to minimize the

temperature swings, which are more rapid up on the wall. In snowier, less sunny climates, you may want to surround the pots with bales of straw or bags of leaves, or to cover them with a plant blanket (sometimes sold to cover early crops of vegetables) that lets in air and light but keeps temperatures a bit more stable. A blanket will also reduce visits from squirrels and deer.

## PLACING THE POTS

Cactus, delospermas, yuccas, agaves, and talinums generally have their growth spurts during weather when temperatures are above 60°F. They'll do best in full sun, especially in the more northern parts of the country. In the far Southwest and the South, succulents in containers may appreciate a little shade during the hottest hours of the day, especially for young plants and during the heat of summer when temperatures pass the 100°F mark.

Pots of sempervivums, lewisias, and some sedums may do very well in full sun in winter, spring, and autumn, while they are in full growth, but they will suffer in the midsummer sun. When they're in pots, you have the option of moving them to a shadier location, such as the north side of a fence or the house. On the other hand a warm, south-facing wall, or an open patio that receives lots of sun, is an excellent place for cactus pots.

## RIGHT PLANT, RIGHT POT

The shape of a pot influences the amount of water available to a plant and the amount forced on the plant roots. Think of a kitchen sponge as representing a fixed amount of soil mix. When lifted horizontally from water, it is like a short but wide pot and holds a large quantity of water. If you pick up the sponge by a corner and hold it vertically, a great deal of water drains out immediately! Similarly, a tall, narrow pot will hold much less water than a low, wide pot with the same volume of soil. The tall pot also has a deeper dry zone of soil at its top, as water evaporates; soil near the bottom of the pot stays moister. Succulents may be grown in either container, but in the taller pot you can water more often without worrying about saturating the top part of the soil or rotting the roots near the surface.

Of course, you'll also choose your pot to complement and accentuate a plant, especially if you are growing a succulent to show or to use as a focal point of your garden or terrace. Do you want a solid-colored pot, maybe cobalt blue, so that the pads of a wine-colored opuntia will contrast with it in winter? Will you choose a rustic look, perhaps of unglazed clay with heavy lines, or a thin porcelain pot with a shiny glaze? Would a textured pot complement the texture of the cactus body? Do you want a pot with painted designs or do you want the succulent itself to provide all the patterns of this little composition?

This wide, shallow saucer holds just enough soil to sustain a colorful arrangement of tender echeverias and kalanchoe.

# TALL VS. WIDE POTS

A tall pot, like a sponge held vertically, has a drier zone at the top and a reserve of moister soil in the lower half of the soil. Plants like cactus may prefer the tall pot when grown in really wet climates, although traditional cactus growers in drier climates usually choose low, wide pots. (This is because many cactus have shallow roots that spread horizontally through the soil.)

In a very dry climate, choose a low, wide pot, where the moisture is more even from top to bottom of the pot. Low pots are perfect for most sempervivums and sedums. Of course, how much rain you have and how often you provide water will influence the shape of the pot you choose, as well.

## PRICKLY POTS

Although you'd think they'd be happier in a tall, dry pot, many cactus are actually grown in relatively shallow containers. This is because they have fairly superficial roots that spread laterally through the soil; they're better able to spread out in a flat pot and would be too restricted in a narrow one.

Also, cactus often do well when under-potted — when the plant seems too large for the pot and the roots are crowded. This crowding results in drier soil in the container, because water is being drawn out of the soil by roots in every square millimeter. Soils in areas of any pot where there are no roots remain moist longer, so if the aim is to have the pot dry out rapidly, it's good not to have excess soil.

*Opuntia fragilis* 'Potato'

Consider whether the glazes and clay colors of a pot pick up some of the colors of the plants, or even of the flowers. You might choose a dark pot to contrast with the white spines of *Grusonia clavata*, or a container with a glaze that has golden flecks to pick up on the golden spines of *Cylindropuntia davisii*. Perhaps you'd select a brilliant cobalt pot and drape chartreuse *Sedum rupestre* 'Angelina' over the side.

You could also follow the form of the plant when choosing a container for it. For instance, a tall pot pairs well with a low cactus whose pads tend to hang downward, creating a waterfall effect, as bonsai artists strive for. If you place a dramatic rock or a piece of driftwood to accentuate a cactus form, select a larger pot than if you were planting the cactus on its own.

### Pots That Last

The durability of a pot through the winter depends largely on the clay and the temperature to which it has been fired. Terra-cotta pots are fired to a relatively low temperature (about 1,922°F). These pots absorb a fair amount of water, so when the temperature drops below freezing, the water in the walls of the pot causes the pot to spauld, or peel, or simply to break. You can recognize these pots because they are either unglazed or are painted in designs. High-fire pots made of stoneware are generally fired to between 2,190°F and 2,350°F. Most absorb very little water after this treatment and thus are much more durable. These pots will frequently have glazes, often shiny, that show drip patterns, but usually are not painted in designs. Any pot will break if it has waterlogged soil when it freezes, simply because the soil expands as the water freezes. The shape of the pot also has an influence on how likely it is to break; a pot with a wide opening at the top allows more room for the soil to bulge upward when it freezes.

There are also pots made of materials other than clay. There are pots carved out of stone or wood, and pots made of a variation of concrete called hypertufa. This is a mix of Portland cement, peat moss, and either perlite or vermiculite, and it is fun to play with. You can make your own containers in various shapes and sizes.

### Topdressing

Succulents in pots benefit from the addition of rock mulches, rocks, and other inert materials, such as marbles, shells, and glass. The mulch keeps moisture from accumulating around the base of the plant bodies and can be used to make a pot look more rustic, more mountainous, or more colorful, all according to your taste.

The gorgeous blue-green rosettes of echeveria are beautifully complemented by the rosy coral flowers and flower stems. It's best brought inside in winter, as it is from central Mexico and not hardy north of Zone 8.

# MAKING HYPERTUFA POTS

HYPERTUFA IS A FORM OF MODIFIED CONCRETE, a combination of Portland cement, peat moss, and a lightweight material such as perlite or vermiculite. When moistened, these dry materials can be formed into pots or larger containers and used for the planting of miniature landscapes. The containers are lighter weight than standard concrete, with its sand and small gravel, and thus easier to move about the yard. Also, the acidity of the peat moss will partly counteract the alkalinity of the cement and will provide a container that is less limey. Hypertufa also withstands freezing and thawing well, as long as the original mixture was strong. I have a number of hypertufa containers that are 30 years old and have never been protected from winter weather.

## MATERIALS

The usual formula for hypertufa calls for approximately equal amounts of Portland cement, peat moss, and perlite by volume.

• **Portland cement.** The greater the quantity of cement in the recipe, the stronger the material. Make sure you get a quality Portland cement. Some cement now sold in the United States is not of good quality, so consider buying from a building supply company.

• **Peat moss.** This should be broken down into fine particles, since any lumps may break later, destroying the container, if not small and coated with the cement mix. You can put the peat moss through a quarter-inch piece of hardware cloth, or simply work it thoroughly with your hands or a hoe.

• **Perlite.** This will show in the container as small white dots; because of this, some folks prefer the look of vermiculite. I like to use a small grade of perlite, since the pieces are then small and show less in the final product.

• **Fiberglass fibers.** These are an optional addition, used to strengthen the final pot. They are available at building companies in small bags. Use about a handful of 2½-inch fibers to a half-wheelbarrow of mix. This is not firm science, but merely an attempt to make a product less likely to break when stressed.

## MAKING THE MIX

Measure the dry ingredients into a wheelbarrow and mix them thoroughly. You'll want to wear a face mask to avoid inhaling airborne particles. It is also advisable to wear rubber gloves since cement is caustic.

Gradually add water to the mix. Be very careful not to get the mix too wet, or the cement's strength will be seriously compromised. You're looking for a texture much like that of creamed cottage cheese. Mix to make sure that all the particles are well coated with the cement slurry.

## PREPARING THE MOLD

The beauty of hypertufa is that you can form it into almost any shape you can manage to engineer — round, square, oval, or free-form. Your hypertufa will be a mucky, slightly sticky cottage-cheese-like substance.

Choose a container with a shape you like. It might be the rounded bottom of a plastic garbage can, a large bowl, or an old enamelware basin. Line the container with plastic sheeting or a large plastic garbage bag, or grease it with motor oil; the aim is to be able to remove the original container after the hypertufa has set. Shapes with sloping sides will be easier to manage, at least in your first sessions.

Pack the moist hypertufa into the container, making sure not to leave large empty spaces. The hypertufa should be about an inch or two thick. Pay attention to the rim, which, after all, will be on the closest display. When you're finished, poke a drainage hole or two with your finger in the bottom of the container.

## CURING THE CONTAINER

Cover the finished form with plastic if the weather is hot or rain threatens. You want the mold to dry neither too slowly nor too quickly. The hypertufa will set in about 24 hours, depending on the outdoor temperature. Do not allow the material to freeze! Test the hypertufa before attempting to remove it from the mold. During the first day or so, the hypertufa will be soft enough for you to carve it, brush a texture into it with a wire brush, or otherwise put your personal mark on it.

Although these are sturdy containers, the rims are the most fragile, so avoid knocking them with rocks, shovels, or, heaven forbid, automobiles. Hypertufa containers also respond poorly to being dropped. Should you have a rim break off, you can try repairing it with some version of cement patch — it will look rustic, but will avoid the pain of transplanting a mature plant or group of plants.

## COMPOSING THE POT PICTURE

Using succulents in pots is an opportunity to compose a symphony of textures and foliage colors, from the tiny leaves of *Sedum hispanicum* and *Talinum okanoganense* to the rounded balls of *Echinocereus* or a huge ball of *Pediocactus simpsonii* or *Coryphantha vivipara*. In even larger pots you could feature a miniature form of *Yucca harrimaniae* or *Agave parryi*.

### Cactus in Pots

I prefer to grow many cactus in pots, where they are isolated from the rampages of the open garden and I am alert to their spines and prickles. Also, they can be weeded more easily in pots (with a long tweezers, available in hobby shops that feature model planes and ships).

I have even seen large pots filled with cactus placed within xeric gardens, where they are more visible because they are raised up, and where they are less readily enmeshed with other plants — from which the gardener will eventually have to disentangle them. This way, they are also limited in how rapidly they can spread. They remain in full light because other perennials don't lean over to shade them (which may prove detrimental in a cloudy climate). At least 100 species of cactus are hardy in Zone 5, and perhaps farther north, especially in pots.

### A Sempervivum Pot

A great way to showcase a few of your favorite sempervivums is to plant them together in a pot. I usually try to find a large pot, perhaps 28 inches long and 12 inches wide — as big as I can find, although it need not be more than 4 to 6 inches deep. I then select three, or five, or at the most seven different sempervivums, arranging the nursery pots around the container to see how the plants look together. I try for good contrast — and for plants that appear different enough that I can keep them distinguished!

Thus, I might put my *Jovibarba* 'Gold Bug', with its stiff leaves heavily touched with yellow tints, next to the dark burgundy *Sempervivum* 'Zephyrine', which is covered with white cobwebbing in spring and early summer. Then I might add the softly fuzzy and twisted rosettes of *S.* 'Whirligig', the small but brightly glowing red 'Jewel Case', and the rounded, blue-white *S.* 'Blue Moon'.

### A Sedum Pot

For an easy but interesting pot near your sidewalk, where it may need to withstand the hazards of snow shovels and passersby, choose a heavy (hard-to-move) pot and set in the colorful *Sedum kamtschaticum* 'Variegatum' as a tall accent plant. Add *S. spurium* 'Red Carpet' at its feet for a year-round dark red display. *Sedum* 'Bertram Anderson' could be added at the base of the planter or on the opposite side, where it will likely be slightly taller than *S. kamtschaticum* and will

provide bright pink flowers toward the end of summer. These plants, all on their own, will fill up to three square feet in the first year and will last in the same pot for many years. Remove the flowering stalks after bloom is done, and occasionally you may want to pinch back one or another plant to keep the overall picture in proportion and the players restrained. There is no easier pot than this to maintain.

For a shady trough, try the foot-tall *Sedum sieboldii* 'Mediovariegatum', its arching stems lightened with pale yellow and white, with the flat, dark green mat of rounded leaves of *S.* 'John Creech'. Add the pale blues of the plump rosettes of *S.* 'Cape Blanco' or 'Harvest Moon'. If your pot is large enough, you can add a golden pad of *S.* 'Ogon' or drape a stem or two of *S.* 'Angelina' over the rim of the pot.

## Matching for Aggression

As in gardens, plants that are combined in pots must be considered for their levels of aggression, lest the more robust force out the more timid. So don't plant a romper like *Sedum* 'Angelina' with a delicate, slow-growing alpine like *Sempervivum arachnoideum*. Use 'Angelina' with a vigorous annual or with a larger, more upright sedum like 'Vera Jameson' or 'Neon'. Or mix it with another ground-cover sedum like 'Voodoo'. Combine in a pot several small growers, such as *Sedum dasyphyllum*, *S.* 'Ogon' and *S.* 'Cape Blanco'. Fairly restrained, clumping sedums, such as *S. middendorffianum* can share a pot with the more vigorous of the sempervivums, such as 'Silverine', 'Agnes', and 'Dream Girl'. Most sempervivums will be fine with most others — except perhaps the smallest selections. Cactus and agaves and the smallest yuccas pair well with ice plants, ground-cover sedums, and talinums as companions in the pot.

ABOVE: The subtle gray shades and small rosettes of *Orostachys furusei* twine about the face mask (created by Barb Horovitz), while the brighter reds of the sempervivum act almost as a rose at her ear.

LEFT: You can drop a pot of golden barrel cactus into the hardy garden scene to add color and drama. Here, the scene setters include *Yucca thompsoniana,* with *Sedum* 'Angelina' at its feet on the left.

# CHAPTER 4

# SUCCULENT GROUND COVERS

**ABOVE:** A rapidly dividing sempervivum can cover a large area of garden at a low level.

**RIGHT:** A fast-spreading ice plant like *Delosperma cooperi* can create sheets of color in season.

Ground covers are found in almost every yard. Though an ambiguous term, *ground cover* usually refers to plants that form dense mats, with leaves close together, usually less than six inches high. A good ground cover should spread well in average soils, vigorous but not to the point of overwhelming other plants. In addition, the plant should grow thickly enough to exclude most annual weeds. It should also have a long season of neat and colorful foliage, of course.

Succulents are among the best ground covers, with sedums and ice plants leading the way. They offer a wider variety of colors and textures, they don't need to be mowed, and they require considerably less water than most common lawn grasses. Flowering is another bonus, in some cases a bright yellow frosting, in others a bright pink or white haze low over the ground.

Try a succulent ground cover around other plants, as a living mulch. Let it fight the weeds while providing a beautiful carpet for rosebushes, lavenders, evergreen trees, or herbs. Plant a succulent ground cover on a slope that is too steep to mow conveniently, or in the strip between the sidewalk and the street where lawn grass is difficult to water properly. Succulents are also a lovely foil for spring bulbs, from crocuses to tulips to daffodils.

## ICE PLANTS: SPARKLING FLOWERS, PLUMP FOLIAGE

Hardy ice plants were introduced into the United States as recently as the 1980s. In California, several genera of ice plants (*Carpobrotus* and *Lampranthus*) line the freeways, brightening the cement and asphalt corridors of the modern human rush with sparkling magenta, yellow, and white flowers. As with anything else that grows readily and in great abundance — even in this winter-wet, summer-dry climate of the coast, where standard perennials and shrubs from more temperate climes would curl up their toes and die — humans have learned to despise this poor plant. It has escaped into the wild in some places, jeopardizing the native flora.

Like the California ice plants, the delospermas originate in Africa. In the 1980s and 1990s, Denver Botanic Gardens turned them into a great bonanza by distributing them freely to nurseries and acquainting the public with them through its publications and display gardens. It first tested *Delosperma nubigenum*, with its apple green foliage and shining yellow flowers. The species proved not only hardy, but also enthusiastic about the soils and climate of Colorado (much deprecated for its clay, alkaline soils, low humidity, and low annual rainfall). This plant prospered, spreading a foot or more from a two-inch plant in a single season, and proving hardy for almost everyone in this Zone 5 climate.

Next tested was the bright pink *Delosperma cooperi*, and soon it was being propagated by the hundreds of thousands and sold at discount retailers. Since then, many more species have been introduced and spontaneous hybrids and sports have been found among the millions of plants being grown,

both from cuttings and from seed. The plants shown here are a few of the best.

I've found that ice plants like a bit more than Denver's 12 to 15 inches of rain per year to really prosper. They will not tolerate sodden conditions, however, so if you live in an area with higher rainfall, give them good drainage. All prefer full sun. Ice plants will survive winter best if they are allowed to dry out a bit in late autumn, so that they are not plump with water. In wetter climates, this may mean that they'll need protection from precipitation and from the late-winter/early-spring weather that leaves the ground frozen while cold rains fall. A deep gravel mulch

LEFT: *Delosperma nubigenum* takes the lowly role, towered over by the six-inch spires of *Sedum reflexum* 'Blue Spruce', with *Opuntia phaecantha* in the background.

RIGHT: *Delosperma cooperi* spills out of tipped pots and onto the ground, mingling with the blues of *Festuca glauca* and the greens of thymes and taller grasses.

may protect them, or a winter blanket of woven row cover (like Reemay). In the wild, these plants grow in grass, among rocks — in many different situations from low plains to the high mountains of the Draakensberg in South Africa.

A winning feature of delospermas is that their mats are generally thick enough to inhibit the growth of weeds, especially the annoying little annuals like portulaca (*Portulaca oleracea*) and spotted spurge (*Euphorbia maculata*). If only there were a ground cover dense enough to exclude crabgrass . . .

### ❀ *Delosperma nubigenum*

Apple green, rounded leaves form a tight mat, blushing to deep red in fall and winter. The mats green up as spring comes on and then they burst into glorious, shiny yellow bloom in spring and early summer. This most hardy of ice plants doesn't tolerate total drought, but will do well with just a little water. It also grows quickly: a plant in a 2½-inch pot will reach 12 inches across in a single season. It does well in both clay-rich and sandy soils. Water it less as winter approaches, and in colder climates plant it on a south-facing slope. Zones 5 to 9.

### ❀ *Delosperma cooperi*

Fast-spreading when happy, to as much as three or four feet across, with inch-long leaves, round in cross section. The large flowers are abundant and a glistening fuchsia. Leaves remain plump in winter, green often flushed with purple, in some situations turning gray-purple. The mat is a bit more open than that of *D. nubigenum*, and is

perhaps more tolerant of heat and drought. Zones 5 to 9.

### ❀ *Delosperma* 'John Proffitt' (Table Mountain)

Introduced by Denver Botanic Gardens and the Plant Select program in 2002, this selection blooms for a longer period and tolerates more moisture than does the similar *D. cooperi*. Its foliage is also more attractive in winter. The flowers are bright pink. Zones 4 to 9.

### ❀ *Delosperma* 'Beaufort West'

This is a smaller plant, not as hardy as *D. nubigenum*, forming a tight clump perhaps six inches across in the first season. The sugary, delicious, sweet pink flowers are about half an inch in diameter. Zones 5b to 10.

### ❀ *Delosperma floribundum* 'Starburst'

The bright pink flowers sport blindingly white centers, making a brilliant accent plant and an astonishing ground cover. This long-blooming, 4-inch-tall plant spreads in a tight mat to about 10 inches wide in the first year. It was a Plant Select introduction from Denver Botanic Gardens in 1998. Zones 5 to 9.

### ❀ *Delosperma* 'Kelaidis' (Mesa Verde)

This plant (thought to be a hybrid between *D. nubigenum* and *D. cooperi*) represents a color break in the species with pastel, salmon-pink flowers. It may be more tolerant of wet conditions than is *D. cooperi*. The flowers are abundant and the lovely

color blends well with other perennials. It is great fun as a ground cover or with diascias (*Diascia*), salvias, coralbells (*Heuchera*), and veronicas. It was named for Panayoti Kelaidis, of Denver Botanic Gardens, who has been deeply involved in the introduction of many ice plants. Zones 5 to 10.

### *Delosperma basuticum* 'Gold Nugget' and 'White Nugget'

These are selections of tight-clumping ice plants, similar to *D. nubigenum* but with even more abundant flowers (yellow and white, respectively). In intensely hot climates, they appreciate a bit of shade. These do not spread as widely as *D. nubigenum*. Zones 4 to 8.

*Delosperma* 'Kelaidis' is a lovely flower color break from the magentas and bright yellows of the genus. It has beautiful peach to apricot flowers with more yellow at the centers. It's named after Panayoti Kelaidis of Denver Botanic Gardens, who has introduced and enthusiastically promoted many of the ice plants currently in cultivation in the United States.

## CREEPING SEDUMS: RELIABLE WORKHORSES

Sedums are a vast and varied tribe of plants, and whole books have been written about this single genus! Fortunately, among them are found some very reliable ground covers. Many of these are widely available, grow easily, and spread well, especially in good garden soils. Prime among these is *Sedum spurium,* willing to spread as much as 12 to 18 inches a year and cover ground up to and around other plants. If it is allowed to romp for a number of years in an intensely planted site, it could create a situation where the gardener has to dig it out. Choose a place for it where it will bring you more pleasure than work.

There are a few overly rambunctious species — such as *Sedum acre* and *S. sexangulare* — that experienced gardeners may never let in the garden gate. Every piece that breaks off forms another clump, and these can easily fill up your garden. They may be "easy to grow" but they are all hell to keep within limits. Beware the aggressive sedum and use it at your peril. Like an attack dog, it may someday turn on you. Choose your site carefully, though, and you may find it helpful between a rock and a hard place.

Like the rapidly reproducing members of any family, these plants have given sedums a reputation for being fast and loose. But most species are much better behaved and have a very useful place in the society of polite garden plants. There is at least one sedum, probably many, that will cover ground in any site your garden offers.

Sweeps of contrasting *Sedum* species can be used to create intriguing patterns as ground covers or (in this image) on green rooftops.

### ✾ *Sedum spurium* 'Red Carpet'

*Sedum spurium* is a reliable, husky, drought-tolerant, much used and very deserving plant. Its leaves are rounded and thick and remain a maroon red throughout the year. To me, 'Red Carpet' is the best of the *S. spurium* selections. In winter the leaves seem reduced, allowing the stems to show and displaying less color. But it begins to grow rapidly when warmer weather arrives in April or May, and forms a solid-colored low mat throughout the growing season. This selection stays dark red during all but the hottest times of the year, contrasting nicely with all the greens of the garden.

It is vigorous on slopes, but also in average garden conditions. Once established, it will tolerate a great degree of drought and neglect. It spreads several inches a year, much more when given extra water and food. In too much shade it will make a mat that is too open to exclude weeds, however, so plant it in full sun.

'Fulvenglut' is another very colorful selection, with tones from orange to red; 'Bronze Carpet' is a bit greener and more orange in its highlights. 'Tricolor' is a fun and popular cultivar, with shades of green, pink, and white. In early, cool weather, the pink tones are especially noticeable. In hot, dry summers, most of the pink is replaced with green. Combine this selection with greener-foliaged ground cover for areas of contrast. Zones 2 to 8.

ABOVE: *Sedum spurium* 'Red Carpet' entwines with one of the ground sages (*Artemisia*), the deep red contrasting with powder blue. These plants can be used as a foil for small spring bulbs, such as crocuses and fritillaries, also.

RIGHT: Leaf shape is almost the only hint that the cultivar 'Tricolor' is also a *Sedum spurium*. It shows more pink in early spring and in late autumn; the summer's heat turns the foliage to green and white.

*Sedum sexangulare, S. anglicum, S. lydium, S. acre,* and others can be a nuisance in a rock garden or among choice perennials, where every tiny leaflet that breaks off quickly forms a new plant. But in the harsh environment of stepping-stones, this sort of *joie de vivre,* elsewhere interpreted as aggression, is just the ticket. Many of these tiny, somewhat weedy sedums have foliage of an especially appealing apple green. They produce a smashing floral display in the dog days of summer — bright yellow in most, although *S. album* flowers are an ivory white. This one takes on deep purple-red tones in the colder months. There is even a very miniature form, should you want to create a miniature landscape.

### ❋ *Sedum spurium* 'John Creech'

This selection tolerates dry shade — that is, not the droughty conditions that eight inches of rain per year present, but still a good deal of drought — and a good deal of shade and the root competition from pines and perhaps even silver maples (*Acer saccharinum*). It is the best selection so far for these conditions. The leaves are deep green, round, and cute. A touch more water and a bit of fertilizer will result in a denser mat and pink flowers. This

Here, a gorgeous form of the blue spruce sedum (*S. reflexum*) and the magenta and green *Delosperma* 'John Proffitt' frame a small clump of *Opuntia fragilis* 'Potato' just budding up to bloom.

is a recent and outstanding introduction from China named for the eminent retired director of the National Arboretum in Washington, D.C, who introduced many treasures from the Orient. Zones 2 to 8.

### ❋ *Sedum makinoi* 'Ogon'

'Ogon' is a recent, yellow-foliaged introduction that brightens those parts of the garden in dappled shade. It holds its flat round leaves parallel to the ground as much as 4 inches high, spreading to about 10 inches in a year. Give it full sun in moist climates, shade or part shade in hot, sunny regions. Although it is somewhat drought-tolerant, it wants some moisture to grow well and look happy. Zones 3 to 8.

### ❋ *Sedum reflexum* 'Blue Spruce'

This is a wonderful, small-scale ground cover for hot dry spots as well as more moderate sites. The short stems (to about five inches high) are a bit lax, but they have a cool and tidy blue tone. The branches arch over their neighbors, giving a nice textural variation to any planting. I have seen them charmingly intertwined with *Sedum hispanicum*, the miniature leaves of the latter contrasting very nicely, and the winter tones of purple and red make a lovely tapestry throughout the winter. This plant is very drought-tolerant. Should it spread beyond its bounds, hoe it out and try to rake (or vacuum!) up every piece, as it propagates without encouragement. Zones 2 to 8.

## PRICKLY CARPETS

Most likely, you've never thought of using cactus as a carpet. No one would want to recline on the pads of prickly pears, but they make excellent ground covers, especially in dry, sunny climates where water is so precious. They are wonderful foils for native western American plants, as well as for plants of Mediterranean origin. Especially attractive and useful are those prickly pears with small pads. Of course, it's best to seek out those with pads that are fairly close together, so that weeds are excluded as much as possible. Colorful blooms are a bonus.

### ❊ *Opuntia fragilis*

This prickly pear has very small pads, and the pads break off easily, leading to the species name *fragilis*. Also known as *O. schweriniana*, it forms a low (one- to three-inch-high) mat of tightly packed, cute little pads. Even in extremely dry spots, the long, plump oval pads spread out to eventually cover as much territory as you will grant them. There is a huge amount of variation in form, including many spineless selections, forms that become red in winter, and those that are less than an inch in diameter. There is also a lot of difference in how fast the mats spread — some achieve 10 inches across in 10 years, some may eventually become six feet in diameter.

There are several selections that have no spines, definitely an endearing trait to this gardener! They are labeled 'Denudata', meaning "naked," although several different selections are sold under this name in the trade. No spines, but watch out for those tiny glochids, the hairlike stickers that are clumped at intervals across the pads. There is a spineless selection that has dark maroon winter color and whose indentations where the glochids are borne much like the eyes of a potato, earning it the name 'Potato'.

The flowers are a fruity pink or yellow in May, although this species may be reluctant to bloom, especially if it doesn't get enough sun. In northern gardens, make sure you give it a sandy or gravelly soil and protect it from any standing water that accumulates around it in rainy weather, especially when the ground is frozen.

The mat inhibits weeds, except perhaps for those pesky grasses that spread by rhizomes. This is the most cold-tolerant cactus, growing as far north as the Canadian Great Slave Lake. Zones 1 to 9.

### ❊ *Opuntia humifusa*

Also known as *O. compressa*, this native of the eastern United States grows from the East Coast to Montana, from Texas to Florida. It has 6- to 8-inch pads, and all the spines and prickles typical of the prickly pear genus. Many forms are nearly spineless, however, forming lush masses of rubbery stems when happy. In some forms the pads are edged with pink in winter. This species usually has deep golden flowers, sometimes with a reddish heart. Use this where no foot traffic is desired! Zones 3 to 8.

### ❊ *Opuntia polyacantha*

A plant native to the Southwest, this can also be used as a ground cover. One selection is a permanently juvenile form called 'Peter Pan'. It has stunning white spines and makes a close white carpet, growing outward a few inches a year. It does not flower, however, remaining permanently in a childlike state. Zones 3 to 9.

LEFT: *Opuntia* 'Peter Pan' never grows up enough to bloom, but its bright white spines make it a real winner. It spreads much more slowly than *O. fragilis* f. *denudata*.

RIGHT: *Opuntia fragilis* f. *denudata*, here in a form collected by Mary Ann Heacock, spreads rapidly to form a ground cover up to 10 feet across.

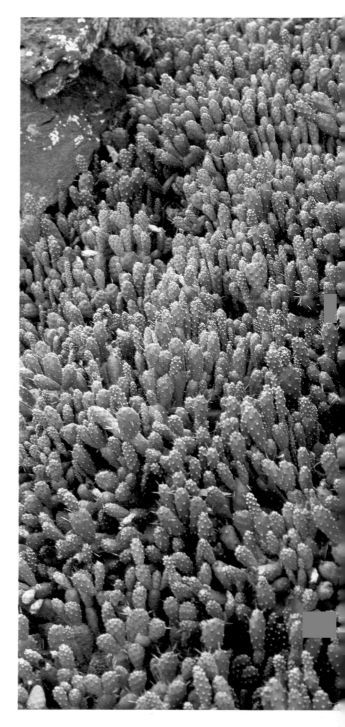

## COVERING GROUND WITH HENS-AND-CHICKS

Sempervivums (hens-and-chicks) can be used to carpet large areas of flat or sloping ground. They do well in clay soils, but they also survive in sandy soils. Because there are so many varieties, it's difficult to generalize about the group as a whole. If you are looking to cover ground quickly, choose the old-fashioned *Sempervivum tectorum* varieties. These have large, usually gray- or olive-green rosettes, as much as five to six inches across. If you place them 8 to 10 inches apart and water them through the summer, you can expect the mats to touch by the end of the season.

You can put sempervivums by themselves in large areas, but this requires quite a few plants to get started. Perhaps more practical is to plant a clump of semps up against steps or a sidewalk, and use sedums for large, open spaces. You can pull apart the sempervivums as they increase in chicks, just stabbing a hole in the soil with a pencil, sticking in the stem of the chick, and crimping the soil back around the chick. If you have trouble with birds or squirrels or rabbits pulling out the newly planted sempervivums, try pinning them

**LEFT:** A form of *Sempervivum arachnoideum*, its biggest rosettes only three-quarters of an inch across, spills around a rock in an almost vertical position. The smaller the rosettes, the slower the rate of growth, so plant accordingly.

**RIGHT:** By combining different cultivars of hens-and-chicks, you can create a lovely picture that enchants the eye with its colors, complexity, and intricacy. Although semps are at their most colorful in spring, they are lovely all year.

down with a landscape staple. (These are often used to pin weed-barrier cloth to the ground or to staple sod until the roots grow in. They should be available at your local hardware store.) For faster results, just do as I do — buy more plants!

In general, the smaller the rosette, the slower the sempervivum spreads. But there are exceptions to this rule. Some varieties that spread rapidly are: 'Ohio Burgundy', 'Agnes', 'Skrocki', some varieties of *S. arachnoideum*, 'Alaska', and 'Drama Girl'. Generally, local nurseries will carry rapidly growing varieties, since the tardy get left behind in most commercial operations. A few small rosettes that keep up through rapid reproduction are the roly-poly types such as *Jovibarba hirta* and *J. arenaria* and the species *S. montanum*.

For good looks, place contrasting types near each other: the fuzzy near the smooth, the bright green near the dark red, and the orange near the gray. This will also aid you in keeping the names

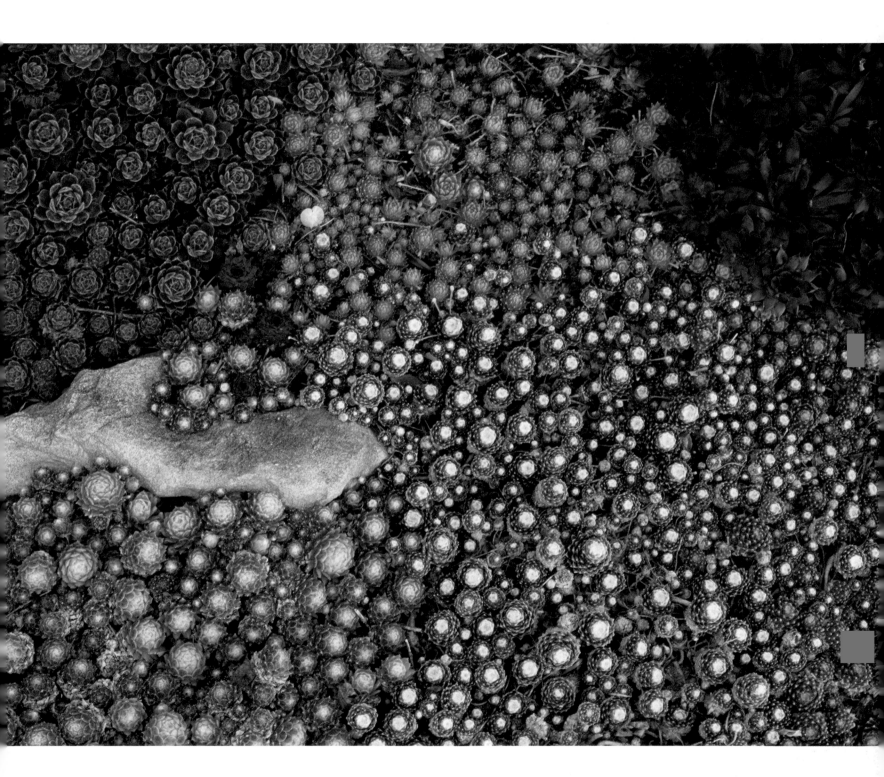

straight, if that's important to you. Some types are more aggressive than others and will tumble through each other and mix like young folks at a party. At some times of the year, especially in May, the types are easier to tell apart. By midsummer, many kinds will have taken on greenish shades that can be tricky to distinguish. Obviously, you would rather have those that maintain good color all year — but it's difficult to tell which they are when you buy them. And they may perform differently in different climates and garden conditions.

My collection of sempervivums stands at more than 200 cultivars and species.

## COLLECTING SEMPS

My mother grew a wide range of varieties in a narrow bed along the west side of the house, retained by a low, 10-inch-wide rock wall along the edge. The sempervivums grew between the rocks of the wall and in the bed above it, mingling and tumbling, presenting a constant counterpoint of interest. It was a carefree planting, the sempervivums pretty much excluding weeds, and it changed through the seasons and through the years, one type winning more space some years, another semp proving more vigorous in others.

I don't admit to being a collector of sempervivums. Once, while shopping at a nursery offering 2,000 varieties, I only bought 120 kinds. Browsing a Web site offering more than 500 varieties, I wrote down only 29 to add to my current holdings of 200 plus. The new ones are different! Honest! At any rate, far be it from me to suggest that one can no longer work new varieties of plants into a garden design without mussing it up. Plants are wonderful, sempervivums are grand, and it seems to me that they like to live together. So collect away! Just occasionally step back and look at the garden as a whole, and see if there is something to be done to pull it all together.

# SUCCULENTS OVERHEAD

A RECENT DEVELOPMENT IN HORTICULTURE is the use of succulents to carpet rooftops, especially flat rooftops. Called green roofs, these are, at their most basic, a shallow layer of soil spread across a specially designed roof and topped with thick colonies of drought-tolerant plants such as sedums and delospermas. Succulents actually keep a roof drier by soaking up rainfall into their plant bodies, sometimes doubling the life of the roof.

A green roof also provides a number of environmental benefits. It insulates and shades the building, which decreases energy expenses. The plants also take in carbon dioxide and give off oxygen, improving the atmosphere in the process. Where a roof is viewed from higher stories of other buildings, it presents a scene of a bright flowery meadow for urban dwellers. In dense cityscapes, green roofs can soak up rain from storms, reducing the runoff and storm-sewer load at street level.

Prime plants for this application are the more aggressive low sedums, such as *Sedum acre, S. reflexum, S. sexangulare, S. hispanicum, S. dasyphyllum,* and *S. album,* as well as the less aggressive but still strong growing *S. spurium, S. kamtschaticum* and its close relative *S. middendorfianum.* Ice plants are also recommended, including *Delosperma* 'Gold Nugget', *D. cooperi, D.* 'Kelaidis', and even the dainty *D. aberdeenense.*

After enjoying widespread popularity in Europe, green roofs have had their American debut in the eastern and northwestern United States, so the plant selection is generally for areas with at least 30 inches of annual rainfall. For sunnier, less moist climates the selection might be modified to include such plants as *Opuntia fragilis, O. aurea,* and all the many varieties and clones of opuntias.

Before you plant your roof, make sure to consult a structural engineer about the amount of weight it can hold. If you decide to try this on your home, please consult a professional! A green roof requires allowance for drainage and thorough waterproofing before installation. Succulents, because they are short and efficient in their use of water, need much less soil than taller perennials and grasses do, so they are a prime choice for planting over your head. For more information about green roofs, turn to Resources, page 147.

# CHAPTER 5

# PERENNIAL COMPANIONS

**ABOVE:** *Yucca rigida* cavorts among statice, blue fescue (*Festuca glauca*), and a blue-leaved dianthus.

**RIGHT:** *Sedum kamtschaticum* has many forms and many close relatives. 'Weihenstephaner Gold' has both abundant flowers and great red winter color.

The beginning gardener often ignores the leaves of new treasures and concentrates on the flowers — when they bloom, which plants bloom together, and the grand, changing overall picture that the flowering of the garden makes. Although many succulents do have glamorous flowers that contribute to the picture, their primary contribution in the perennial border is one of texture and substance.

Succulents offer not just variation in foliage color and shape, but also a change in texture to the perennial garden picture. The leaves of most perennials are pretty much flat (although they may curve a bit), but the succulent leaf is heavier and more shapely, and gives the plant a new aspect, just as a sketch done in charcoal thickens the lines that could have been laid down in pen and ink. Succulent leaves, thick with water and flesh, add a third dimension to the scene. In this way, succulents give you another factor to consider in how you place plants next to each other, another opportunity to weave a bulkier thread into the garden tapestry.

## SHORT AND UP FRONT

I like to change the look of my perennial border from time to time by redesigning the front edge. Why not dig out those dianthus that looked so good two years ago and try a new color of *Sedum spurium*, maybe 'Fulvenglut', with its harmonious reds, bronzes, and greens, or one of the dark maroon varieties like 'Voodoo'? Or add the bright color of *Sedum rupestre* 'Angelina', that hot chartreuse lass, next to a lavender, pink, or white creeping phlox. It sure will shake up the color scheme.

LEFT: *Sedum sieboldii* can easily be recognized by its rounded, scalloped leaves, in threes along the stem, and by the red rims on each leaf. Growing here with *Festuca glauca*, it does well in part sun or light shade.

RIGHT: *Sedum spurium* 'Red Carpet' is a bit greener in late summer, but is the best variety to hold the red color. It looks great with the blue green foliage of erodium or the lavender of *Aster* 'Wood's Dwarf Blue'.

I smile at the sight of the narrow but plump leaves and floppy stalks of 'Angelina' in front of the stately, wide dark foliage of peonies, too (either a variety that stands up well or staked in a ring). Another plant with bold foliage that contrasts well with 'Angelina' is that great, long-lived, underutilized hero of the border *Dictamnus* (bringing along its unfortunate common name, gas plant), standing so erect and proud, its body of rich green leaves held so upright. Blue border clematis (*Clematis integrifolia*), its leaflets wide at the base and gracefully drooping, the furry animal–like leaves of lamb's ears (*Stachys*), or the rugose, yellow-green leaves of foxgloves (*Digitalis*) — all look delightful near this sedum. The goal is to stimulate the eye by juxtaposing textures, to show off the quality of each plant by contrasting it so closely in the garden painting.

Another whimsical contrast is that of strappy bulb foliage over a low mat of the crisp round leaves of *Sedum spurium*. Try one of the alliums, like the glaucous-leaved curly onion (*Allium senescens*), or an early-spring-blooming one like the wide, blue-green leaves and giant lollipop-like inflorescence of *A. karataviense*. As a matter of fact, the low sedums and ice plants are the perfect cover for the earliest spring flowers in the perennial border, the crocuses, reticulate iris (*Iris reticulata*), and squills (*Scilla*), and the glorious species tulips (*Tulipa humilis, T. batalinii, T. greggii,* and *T. wilsonii,* to name but a few).

There are a great number of low succulents that are appropriate for the front of a bed. The bright flowers may be flashy and shining stars in the border (as are the ice plants) or subdued — just "good soldiers" (many sedums fall into this group). The succulents act as excellent fillers, covering the bare ground among larger plants, allowing the gardener to mulch with plants, excluding weeds while providing color and interest in spring and adding a touch of green, yellow, or red to the winter scene. None will tolerate foot traffic, however, as their leaves are crushed when stepped upon. Some of the border succulents keep up their good looks well into late autumn and start again early in the spring (*Sedum spurium* and *S.* 'Angelina', for example), but most are quite retiring in midwinter.

### Spreading Sedums

Unfortunately, *Sedum album, S. sexangulare,* and *S. acre* have given sedums a reputation for reproducing too freely. But most species restrain themselves quite well, and have a very useful place in the garden.

### ❀ *Sedum spurium*

Several widely available sedums grow easily, especially in good garden soils. Prime among these is *Sedum spurium*, a willing ground cover that spreads as much as 12 to 18 inches a year, covering the areas up to and around other plants. In some situations, it may spread faster than desired. Try restricting it by hoeing, or use an edging material to keep it in check. In a small area, a rock may be enough to restrict its growth. Or you may wish to oppose it with an equally vigorous companion, such as woolly thyme or creeping veronica. There are several lovely forms of this mid- to dark green creeper, with its inch-long leaves and pink flowers.

*Sedum spurium* is also a kindly companion for herbs, such as lavender, *Ballota*, or

*Teucrium*, and for the shrubby, upright thymes — *Thymus richardii* 'Peter Davis', *T. × citriodorus*, or *T. camphoratus*. The herbs are almost woody at the base, forming little shrubs; the soft, fleshy succulents wrap around their feet and clothe the ground beneath and between them. The succulents form a happy backdrop for annual herbs too, such as Chinese lanterns and dark-leaved basil. Herbs and succulents can likewise make a wonderful combination in a xeric garden.

'Tricolor' has variegated leaves, each a bit different. In fall and spring, pinks show up near the center of the plant, providing the third color. If summer is cool and moist, the pinks linger longer; hot weather seems to bring the greens to the fore.

The spooky, dark red 'Voodoo' is said to retain good maroon and dark red foliage through most of the year, but for my money, I think 'Red Carpet' is the best of the reds and shows much less green at midsummer and even in early spring. All the varieties of *Sedum spurium* largely retreat after hard frost and show more of the round, succulent tan stems during this season. Sooner or later, tiny new leaves and shoots emerge,

huddled close to the ground, ready to spring into growth come warm weather.

'Bronze Carpet' has more orange overtones and more weeks during which green predominates in its patch of color. 'Dragon's Blood' is an older variety with red tones.

In addition to the plain green *Sedum spurium*, there are new varieties being introduced every year. All these varieties have pink flowers; in general, the darker the foliage, the deeper pink the flowers. Zones 4 to 8.

### Sedum rupestre 'Angelina'

This striking sedum is lime green to yellow in spring and summer and turns to a shocking orange-red in autumn. The tips of each leaf are particularly colorful and most intense when the plant is grown in full sun. Most plants bear small clusters of yellow flowers in summer, at the tips of curving, 10-inch-high stalks. Even if yours don't bloom, the foliage is at least as decorative as the flowers. This sedum may be grown in average to very dry conditions, and it readily breaks off and roots itself. If deer wander across the garden, you will see this plant popping up all around its original site, broken off and then spread by hooves. However, it is very easy to pull out by hand, should you acquire too much. Although I have been growing this for only a couple of years, I detect in it a tendency to become rambunctious if given a rich soil with plenty of water. I have underplanted it with checkered lilies (*Fritillaria meleagris*), but as it becomes more vigorous, I begin to think of short, scarlet botanical tulips as appropriate companions. Zones 3 to 8.

LEFT: *Sedum rupestre* 'Angelina' can vary from greenish yellow to yellow orange. It's easy and willing to grow with yuccas and agastaches.

RIGHT: Nestled in with *Veronica liwanensis,* this planting of 'Angelina' is preparing to bloom, lifting graceful, nodding stems still touched with winter's orange hues.

### Delospermas

The spectacular flowers of the ice plants are wonderful at the front of the border, surpassing even the beauty of their evergreen or summer-green foliage. Large flowers, often more than an inch across, come in sparkling bright colors — yellow (*D. nubigenum, D.* 'Gold Nugget'), magenta-pink (*D. cooperi*), pink with a white eye (*D. floribundum* 'Starburst'), baby pink (*D.* 'Beaufort West'), and apricot (*D.* 'Kelaidis'). All need full sun. Some do best with a little additional water (*D. nubigenum*), some are very drought-resistant (*D. cooperi*). *Delosperma cooperi* may seem to disappear entirely in winter; in milder climates or years, it retains its foliage through the season. *Delosperma nubigenum* has beautiful dark maroon foliage in cold weather, but will not overwinter if it is very wet going into winter. All the ice plants require well-drained soil in moist climates, although they may perform well in clay or on sand in the droughty states of the Southwest. Many do not survive in Zone 3 or 4, though they are worth trying.

The blue-flowered *Veronica liwanensis* is well matched with *Delosperma cooperi*. Both are enthusiastic spreaders when watered moderately, and they look lovely when they sprawl across each other.

### Edging with Hens-and-Chicks

Clumps of sempervivums can be used between perennials at the front of a bed or tumbled among rocks that edge a perennial border. For this application, choose the larger semps, from the common *S. tectorum* to large-rosetted varieties like 'Commander Hay', a large red-and-green variety that grows up to six inches across. For a purple effect, try 'Plum Rose', which is quite vigorous. An older variety, 'Silverine' is quite large and silvery blue; 'Lavender and Old Lace' is another that may give you the weight and mass you are looking for, and its orchid overtones are especially beautiful in May.

Local garden centers tend to grow the selections of sempervivums that are most vigorous in pots, perhaps not the most colorful but suitable to the edge of perennial borders. Most semps will tolerate other plants overgrowing them a bit, so you can use these near low perennial geraniums such as *Geranium cinereum*, dwarf irises like *Iris tectorum*, diascias (*Diascia integerrima*), and perennial herbs like germanders (*Teucrium*) and thymes, or annual herbs like basil and parsley. However, do take time to clear the foliage of other plants from over the sempervivums toward the middle of the season and into the fall, so they have time to store up sun energy and to tighten their rosettes before winter. Pull off any extra "chicks" to share with friends.

### SUCCULENT COMPANIONS

Plants can be used together not only to create wonderful scenarios of color and texture, but for other garden functions, too. *Sedum kamtschaticum* and its relatives *S. floriferum* and *S. middendorffianum* are sturdy and can be planted on either side of floppier plants to help keep them upright — some of the dianthus and coralbells might be contained this way, and their flowers will show to advantage against the crisp, green foliage of the sedum.

You can use the late-blooming sedums to fill in gaps where earlier-blooming plants have been cut back. For instance, 'Autumn Joy' and 'Frosty Morn' are just reaching their full height and coming into spectacular flower when bee balms have finished (and are becoming covered with powdery mildew). The sedums will fill in space nicely after the bee balms are cut back almost to the ground. All the border sedums are excellent for this purpose, and for extending bloom into late summer at the front of the bed. Voila! Since these plants seem to live long lives, you won't have to replace them, as you would mulch. And when you add another flower bed in a year or two, you can take divisions from this one.

# STARS OF THE BROWN SEASON

MORE AND MORE PEOPLE ARE LOOKING TO THE GARDEN FOR PLEASURE, beauty, and serenity throughout the year. As the winter season has become less severe in the last 20 years, more and more areas of the northern United States have longer periods without snow. I refer to this as the "brown season," and I define it as the period from when the leaves fall until snow covers the ground. It also includes the weeks or months after the snow melts and before spring flowers and golden-green leaves appear to cheer us. In many parts of the country, there seem to be many brown periods that alternate with weeks of snow. In these months, the perennial garden lies devastated, either cut back to the ground by frost and the gardener's shears, or a twiggy mass of spent stems and withered flowers awaiting spring cleanup.

Some succulents, such as the tall sedums, disappear underground with other perennials of the border. But there are a few succulents that truly do provide year-round interest. For winter plant amusement, and the stimulation of your mind and heart, try to include the following in your garden.

*DELOSPERMA CONGESTUM* IN SUMMER

*DELOSPERMA CONGESTUM* IN SPRING

**Fabulous fall hues.** Four closely related sedums — *Sedum cauticola* 'Lidakense', *S. cauticola* 'Bertram Anderson', and *S. sieboldii* brighten the late summer and early autumn with vivid pink spots of floral color and with their hazy gray foliage suffused with purple hues. The purple foliage and stems of *Sedum* 'Vera Jameson' will pick up the yellows and oranges of the azaleas' fall leaves and delight you in the sunny days of Indian summer. After the bloom is past, the broad flower heads turn bronzy and continue the autumnal theme.

Sempervivums also change color with the weather and, since they come in so many shapes, sizes, and colors, they can be combined in endless ways to delight you through the cold months. Try a fuzzy-leaved lavender rosette next to a tightly curled roly-poly *Jovibarba arenaria* type. Or plant a deep purple or red one next to a yellow-tinged type such as 'Limberg' or 'Gold Bug'. The rosettes of most selections become tighter in cold weather, more open in summer. A large pot planted with three or five different varieties, chosen for contrasting colors and textures, will provide you with a changing scene through the cold weather. As winter progresses into spring and then summer, the concert of colors will shift and change, like a kaleidoscope in slow motion.

**Sculptural snow-catchers.** Agaves are magnificent at all times of the year, but they are newly revealed in their symmetrical glory by drifting snow that outlines each leaf with white. In the winter garden, they look both improbable and solidly real, huddled, stout and blue, as though some chubby dwarves

*AGAVE PARRYI*

83

had sat down in your garden and frozen still in place, awaiting spring thaws. Agaves are simply majestic, winter or summer, great stalwart succulents, adding highly valuable plant sculpture to the horticultural scene.

Tree yuccas are extraordinarily impressive in winter, lifting sharp balls of spearlike foliage into the air, providing an effect almost like that of a palm tree here in the North — where palms seldom venture. For blue color, try *Yucca rostrata*, the leaves abundant, the rosettes very full and almost always very well-rounded. A single plant will change the entire aspect of the garden, providing a focal point and a beautiful form throughout the darkest months of the year. I haven't seen one decorated with Christmas lights yet, but who knows?

If you like a touch of yellow, *Yucca thompsoniana* may be your choice. The tips of the leaves trend toward yellow-green in the winter. This is a plant that can have several rounded heads on stubby, thick branches. It can break in heavy snows; dust it off during heavy, wet snowstorms, or prop up the side branches.

**Color in winter.** In containers or gardens with nooks and crannies, *Delosperma*

'Hogan' is an absolute must for its wintry burgundy color. The tiny, rounded green leaves of summer snap into color change with the cool nights of August and September. The intoxicating wine color remains through May to serve as a striking backdrop to tiny, pure white flowers. It grows well with sempervivums, so why not try it with a variety that has very white centers, like 'St. Cloud' or 'Downland Queen'?

*Sedum rupestre* 'Angelina', after it lifts its lilting bloom stems like golden periscopes, continues to delight with its bright chartreuse branches. Then Jack Frost visits one night and suddenly 'Angelina' blushes to orange and deep pink tones, with the gaiety of yellows still buried deep in the mats. Eventually winter reaches most of the plant, and this maid continues to delight throughout the cold season whenever exposed by the flight of snow cover.

Also consider the winter-wine pads of *Opuntia* 'Dark Knight'— almost black and stuck with silver, pinlike spines — or *Opuntia* 'Coombe's Winter Glow', which begins autumn in shades of raspberry and tawny, then matures to a more uniform wine color in winter. The pads in this season are horizontally crinkled (like your Uncle Rodney's poor brow after years working as a bartender nights, fixing flats during the day). The pads are both ornamental and amusing, on close examination and at a distance, where they show as bright patches against white drifts and hummocks of snow. In summer, the pads revert to smooth, succulent blue-green, and in early June shiny flowers of raspberry-pink proclaim that life is good.

OPUNTIA PHAEACANTHA 'DARK KNIGHT' IN EARLY SPRING

*CYLINDROPUNTIA SPINOSIOR*

**Refractors of light.** The shrubby cholla form with its bristling spines is most dazzlingly embodied in the shining silver-sheathed forms of Whipple's cholla (*Cylindropuntia whipplei*). It is amazing in the winter sun, even when surrounded by snow (in fact, there's an especially lovely new selection called 'Snow Leopard'), as crystalline as twigs encased in clean ice on the day after an ice storm, when the sun appears and scatters blinding sparks of light through the world outside. And in the gray days when January has forgotten to dazzle us, Whipple's cholla remains to cheer us with its pure brightness. Place this where sun will shine through it and remind you to rejoice!

**Animated characters.** As winter cold comes on, the pads of *Opuntia basilaris* curve and twist counterclockwise around the plant's central axis and then lie down against the earth, as if sentient and chilly, almost like a small dog or a cat! Many varieties of this species, and of the very similar-appearing *Opuntia aurea,* also take on a rosy glow around the edges of the pad. Nor do they have many spines. Who could ask for a more charming winter companion? (Well, perhaps it would be nice if they could warm our feet!)

## COMPACT SEDUMS

The crisp, short mounds of the *Sedum kamtschaticum* group, including its close relatives *S. middendorffianum* and *S. floriferum*, are used across northern North America, as they are widely available, easy-to-please plants. They hold their mid-green or variegated branches sturdily upright, 8 to 12 inches high, and can be used between more sprawling front-of-the border plants to add mass and continuous, carefree good looks.

### ❋ *Sedum kamtschaticum* var. *floriferum* 'Weihenstephaner Gold'

This species is highly variable, often lumped with the very similar *Sedum middendorffianum*, and the two come in many, many forms that are worthy of growing in the garden. This particular selection has good winter color, remaining from heavy frost until spring in dense clusters of short, dark red stems just above the ground. In summer it is a rounded five- to eight-inch-tall mound of stout branches bearing thick mid-green leaves with softly toothed margins. The flowers form a bright dome of golden yellow. It works well in front of short lilies, next to icy-foliaged pinks (*Dianthus*), cushion mums, dwarf asters, and coralbells (*Heuchera*). This species will increase in diameter, but slowly, and is never invasive, although it may do a bit of self-sowing.

*Sedum kamtschaticum* 'Variegatum' has yellow and white tones on the leaves, lively in summer but is not as attractive as the former selection in the off-seasons. Zones 3 to 8.

### ❋ *Sedum tatarinowii*

At 8 to 10 inches tall, this plant produces a light green mound of branches with heavily toothed leaves. In late summer, it is covered with dainty white or pale pink flowers —an airy effect for a sturdy and substantial plant. It does well in rock garden soils and will likely thrive anywhere its roots aren't too moist. Try it at the front of the border with mat veronicas (*Veronica pectinata, V. prostrata*, or *V. liwanensis*) or creeping thymes where it will meet their aggression with a steady companionship and not be driven out. Likewise, it supplies a foliage contrast for lamb's ears (*Stachys byzantina*), large-leaved salvias (*S. argentea, S. sclarea*), foxgloves (*Digitalis*), or bear's breeches (*Acanthus*). Zones 3 to 8.

LEFT: *Sedum kamtschaticum* var. *floriferum* is one of many similar plants in the trade, including *S. middendorffianum* and *S. floriferum*.

RIGHT: The tiny teeth on these very small leaves and the masses of slender twigs combine to give *Sedum tatarinowii* an airy look.

## STURDY BORDER SEDUMS

After the glories of spring wildflowers and bulbs, after midsummer's lilies, day-lilies, bee balms, and daisies, as the hues of asters and chrysanthemums take over the garden's palette, the sturdy and reliable *Sedum spectabile* and all its cousins take center stage. These sedums emerge in late spring as clumps of fleshy, succulent, blue-gray leaves and slowly gain stature as the plants around them in the border come in and out of flower.

Then in late August the sedums send up large inflorescences of pink to white to coppery flowers, attractive as buds, lovely as flowers, and still of great interest after flowering is over, holding up their stiff umbrellas for admiration from afar. They are hybrids or selections from *Sedum telephium*, *S. spectabile*, and *S. cauticola* (many of which are now reclassified as the genus *Hylotelephium*). All are visited by butterflies, honeybees, and many other insects, bringing together a fine garden party in late summer, should you feel a bit wistful at the onset of fall and want company.

Like other border perennials, these sedums die back to the ground during the winter months. Their lovely, plump new leaves emerge as the hyacinths are bloom-ing, and can be used to cover the ripen-ing foliage of bulbs, as the sedums quickly gain height in May. All are hardy in Zones 3 to 8.

### ❁ *Sedum* 'Autumn Joy'

Introduced in 1955, this is the oldest and best-known sedum here in the United States, a plant that needs no staking and knows no disease or insect plague. The flowers are rosy pink and borne in large, flat heads as much as five inches across. The leaves are blue-green and heavily toothed.

It is reliable, easy to divide, and grows splendidly in a wide range of conditions. One of the great stalwarts of the perennial border, it can also be used as a stand-alone plant in a large sweep — as long as it is not trampled, for it does object to being walked upon. It reaches 28 to 36 inches tall.

If you live in an area with rainfall beyond 35 inches per year, 'Autumn Joy' and its relatives may flop, especially when planted in shade or even half shade. Don't give it any supplemental water, and plant it in full sun — on a slope, if possible.

Some say 'Indian Chief' is identical to 'Autumn Joy', but in my experience, 'Indian Chief' is much more coppery. In late summer, it spreads an umbel of tightly clustered, burnt-orange flowers, maintaining strong, blue-green foliage, striking in itself.

### ❁ Sedum 'Neon'

This selection is shorter than either of the above, at about 15 inches, and the flowers are a brilliant shade of magenta-pink. It is just as upstanding and just as tolerant of poor soil, and it may fit better with your range

LEFT: *Sedum* 'Autumn Joy' is probably the most widely grown and loved sedum, shown here with *Aster* 'October Skies'.

RIGHT: From the same group of many hybrids and selections comes *Sedum* 'Neon', a shorter plant with knock-your-socks-off color.

of perennials than the taller sedums do. Try it with cushion mums (*Chrysanthemum* × *morifolium*) and dwarf asters to brighten up the garden as children return to school. Or use it to generate late-summer interest among plants that have gone all green.

'Brilliant' and 'Carmen' are similar, but slightly different in height and color. It is perhaps best to purchase these in flower. And remember, height and bloom time may be different in a nursery plant than it is in your garden.

**ABOVE:** The ruby stems of *Sedum* 'Matrona' provide a striking contrast in the garden.

**RIGHT:** A red-leaved dahlia provides the perfect backdrop for *Sedum* 'Frosty Morn'.

### ✿ *Sedum* 'Frosty Morn'

A lovely, variegated-foliage plant of the same group of cousins, 'Frosty Morn' has thick green-and-white leaves. It reaches 12 to 18 inches tall, depending on your conditions. It tolerates warmth, like most members of this group, but perhaps not as much drought as its greener pals. If the weather is cool, the flowers will be light pink, but if summer is still hot, look for white. In very high and sunny climates, where drought can interrupt the forward progress of the summer garden, the light-foliaged and white-flowered selections like this one seem to sunburn more easily, and they look a bit faint around the edges.

'Stardust' has white flowers and light green leaves. 'Green Expectations' is for those of you who like to throw in a surprise for your friends and visitors: the thick, bluish leaves are joined by heavy, broccoli-like clusters that open to yellow-green flowers. Is it a flower or a vegetable? I have a similar reaction to green tulips. Great contrast, great interest, and, as usual, easy to grow.

### Dark Purple Selections

A number of maroon-foliaged introductions have come out in the last 10 years, including 'Matrona', 'Möhrchen' ('Little Moor'), and 'Purple Emperor'. There is some confusion about these names; not all nurseries seem to have the same plant called the same name. And is 'Möhrchen' the same as 'Little Moor'? Whatever you call them, use the dark thick foliage to contrast with the ferny blue-greens of yarrow (*Achillea*) or seseli (*Seseli*). Or plant them as a backdrop for the airy flowers of *Gaura lindheimeri* or coralbells (*Heuchera*).

You could also create an entire garden that specializes in contrasting dark foliage with green, using purple smoke tree (*Cotinus coggygria* 'Royal Purple'), purple-leaved ninebark (*Physocarpus opulifolius* 'Diablo'), any of the lovely dark barberries (*Berberis thunbergii* f. *atropurpurea*), and dark-foliaged Joe-pye weed (*Eupatorium rugosum* 'Atropurpureum'). Add one of the dark *Sedum spurium* selections, such as 'Red Carpet' or 'Voodoo', to extend the intoxifying effect of wine-red forward to the edge of the bed. If you plant checkered fritillary (*Fritillaria meleagris*) under the mats of 'Voodoo' at Halloween, will your friends be spooked or charmed when the bulbs come up next spring?

## SEDUMS FOR SHADE

Although most succulents delight in full sun and tolerate low water, there are a few that are adapted to the shade. Some even thrive in dry shade, that very challenging environment so often created by large trees that both intercept rainfall and soak up any available soil moisture with their massive root systems.

### ✺ *Sedum populifolium*

This plant is something of a curiosity. It's almost woody at the base, with many branches appearing there and forming a 15-inch-high clump, leaves thick and green as a miniature rhododendron — only it's a thousand times easier to grow! It is semi-evergreen in all but the harshest climates. The flowers are white, sometimes with a pinkish cast, but go by scarcely noticed in most gardens. It creeps by underground runners at a moderate rate: just slow enough not to be a bother, but reliable enough that you can share with your gardening friends. It needs a bit of shade in most climates and prefers at least a little moisture, though it is surprisingly tough. Green from late spring until heavy frosts lay it low, *Sedum populifolium* provides a cheerful background to daffodils and primroses and the woodland foxgloves and astilbes, and a foliage contrast to the many hostas. It's also easy to propagate and not a bit fussy. Zones 3 to 8.

*Sedum populifolium* is easy to grow in half-day or full shade and is long-lived. Use it as a backdrop to primroses, or as a counterpoint to one of the coralbells with bright red or lime green foliage.

### ✺ *Sedum sieboldii*

With its arching stems and late-summer pink flowers, *Sedum sieboldii* is a graceful and useful addition to the shady garden; it looks particularly nice at the base of a rock or tree trunk. The leaves are rounded and scalloped and rimmed with red — a thoroughly lovely plant. Of Japanese origin, these plants reach about nine inches tall and are slightly less vigorous than other sedums, needing moisture as well as shade. If they thrive in your garden, rejoice! This species can also be displayed in hanging pots, because its natural tendency to arch will carry it over the rims.

The cultivar 'Mediovariegatum' claims *S. sieboldii* heritage, but it is a larger plant, with stems up to 14 inches tall. The leaves seldom show red rimming, but are instead decorated with a bright yellow center stripe or splotch. This plant is a charmer, popping out brightly like a patch of dappled sunlight in the woodland garden. Watch out for stems that revert to plain green, and be sure to remove them. Like the type, the variegated form seems none too vigorous — or perhaps I just haven't made it happy yet. This form has pink flowers, but is really grown more for its foliage than for its flowers. Plant it with other variegated woodlanders, such as variegated

Jacob's ladder (*Polemonium* 'Brise d'Anjou'), Japanese painted fern (*Athyrium niponicum* var. *pictum*), and variegated rock cress (*Arabis* 'Variegata'). Pair it with bicolored hostas to brighten a bed of primulas, daffodils, astilbes, woodland iris, and foxgloves, and you will have created a lively scene throughout the growing season. Zones 4 to 8.

### ❋ *Sedum spurium* 'John Creech'

Selected from a strain of *Sedum spurium* found in China, this tough plant will grow at the feet of a pine tree where competition for water and light are fierce. It has neat, rounded leaves forming a four-inch-high mat. The modest flowers are pale pink. Give it a bit of extra compost and water, and it will grow to quite a thick mat. Combine it with the variegated *Lamium maculatum* selections such as 'White Nancy' or 'Beacon Silver' to achieve a contrast under trees. Zones 3 to 8.

Yummy yellow variegation on *Sedum sieboldii* 'Mediovariegatum' lets the gardener bring light into the woodland garden. This is the perfect companion to green or blue hostas, astilbes, and bergenias.

## CACTUS IN THE PERENNIAL GARDEN

Cactus have particular needs, especially in cold climates. They want superior drainage and full sun, and they won't tolerate too much water. Cactus don't want heavy foliage hanging over them, or to be crammed in among dense plants. They need good air circulation and low humidity. If you want to mix them in with other perennials, then, you must provide for their special growing requirements and choose appropriate companions.

At the same time, cactus offer a desirable contrast of form to most other perennials. The wide, thick pads of opuntias, with their egg-shaped prickly pear fruits, are a wonderful contrast to the texture of most other perennials. And the flowers are unbeatable for brilliance of color.

If the conditions of your perennial garden are the same as those required by cactus — dry and sunny — you can mix them right in. The five-foot spread of a prickly pear looks terrific next to the airy spikes of agastache or a drought-tolerant veronica, or any of a myriad penstemons, from the gorgeous *Penstemon pseudospectabilis* to the beefy clumps of the Mexicali hybrids. Oriental poppies (*Papaver orientale*) and the brilliant horned poppies (*Glaucidium cornuta*) are right at home with cactus. Cactus are likewise boon companions to any of the dryland herbs, such as lavender (*Lavandula*), horehound (*Ballota*), culinary sage (*Salvia officinalis*), oregano (*Origanum vulgare*), and the small, shrubby thymes (*Thymus*).

If you have a more mesic (moderately moist) perennial garden but you still long for cactus, try growing them in large pots set into the garden. This way, you can give them more-rapid drainage, at the same time raising them above the overhang of neighboring foliage. Another considerable benefit is that if the cactus are growing in pots, you are less likely to come upon them unexpectedly while you are weeding or tidying up in among other perennials; you'll know just where the cactus are. This may give you a more relaxing gardening experience, but still enable you to enjoy the beauty of cactus in the garden.

LEFT: *Opuntia engelmannii* has large blue pads and one of the best fruit displays of the hardy prickly pears. In the foreground is *Calylophus hartwegii* and taking the backseat is *Salvia greggii* 'Wild Thing'.

RIGHT: *Opuntia* 'Coombe's Winter Glow' is renowned for its rosy flowers and husky vigor, but especially for its deep maroon winter color. Here, it's displayed in a carefree planting with *Salvia* 'Blue Hill' and *Centranthus ruber* (Jupiter's beard).

# XERIC GARDEN DESIGN

THE LANDSCAPES of the American West may not be luxurious, but they are extraordinarily majestic. They speak to the heart through their sense of sky and space, rock and slope. The challenge of re-creating the style of the Southwest is to capture and regenerate this aesthetic sense through the use of the plants. It is no small challenge.

Succulents such as agaves and yuccas are both an integral part of the Southwestern landscape and a nearly inescapable part of the truly xeric garden, since they offer so much year-round interest, height, and character. A stunning garden can be made with *only* these and other succulents — and many a stunning garden can be composed with these and the added elements of dryland perennials and annuals. Equally, if you think that yuccas, agaves, and cactus are too stereotypical for your garden, you can use other succulents presented in this book and exclude those traditional elements. Here are a few suggestions for the design of your xeric garden:

**LEFT:** Peckerwood Garden, in Hempstead, Texas, uses masses of gravel to offer succulents proper drainage and to visually unify the landscape. Brightly colored walls mark the entrance to the main garden.

**Add height and mass first.** Choose a tall plant or two to achieve height in your design. You might use a tree yucca, a dwarf or character evergreen (such as a pinyon or ponderosa pine or even a juniper), or perhaps a cholla (*Cylindropuntia*). Even a few landscape rocks can add a lot of substance to your design, while also suggesting permanence. If you can, add some topography to your garden by siting it on a slope or building up a berm.

Once you have decided on the placement of the largest components of your design, you can group other plants around them. I find it useful to group the next-largest plants, either moving outward from the tallest, or grouped to form a new, smaller mass in another part of the garden. You can then add shorter plants between and around the edge.

**Consider adding a gravel mulch.** Many succulents benefit from having dry crowns. Rock mulch can help keep succulents from contact with moist soil and from any soil-splash that may occur during heavy rainfall. Even a quarter of an inch of gravel spread across the soil will improve conditions. Rock mulch cools the soil and keeps it open, allowing rain to penetrate rather than to run off. But cactus, agaves, and yuccas will tolerate, even enjoy, a much thicker layer of mulch — two inches or even six inches. In climates that receive 35 inches or more of rain in a year, these plants can even be grown in 12-inch-deep sharp sand or pea-sized gravel.

Now you have probably seen rock mulches that you found disturbing, if not repulsive. Large sweeps of rough gravel — often red or black scoria or glaring white quartz — may give you an arid and desperate feeling, like that ragged man crawling across the desert sand in cartoons. Using gravel that matches your larger rocks will lend more harmony to the garden scene. Gravel of mixed and smaller sizes can also seem friendlier and more natural than large chunks. But primarily, if you want to create a garden, you'll do well to simply add more plants (and a larger variety of them), rather than to have large expanses of plain old gravel. Most people like plants better than gravel, after all. And gravel doesn't bloom!

**Pair with perennials and annuals.** As the garden writer Eleanor Perenyi once wrote, "Gardening is the slowest of the performing arts." This is especially true for xeric gardens, which, compared to the perennial garden or a bed of annuals, don't change much through the seasons — no great numbers of new flowers appear suddenly overnight, no plants grow up from low clusters of stems to taller flowering plants, no sweeps of color appear and disappear. It's certainly a more static gardening experience.

So why not add perennials and annuals to the xeric succulent garden? In fact many new plants that are tolerant — nay, *desirous* — of dry conditions have been introduced in the last 20 years. There is an array of agastaches, salvias, evening primroses (*Oenothera*), and penstemons that can provide highly complementary color to the succulent garden. Blackfoot daisy (*Melampodium*) and *Zinnia grandiflora* are natural, native additions. Visit the Web site of High Country Gardens for ideas (see Resources, page 149); this Santa Fe, New Mexico, garden center is a leader in making available plants that thrive in Southwestern conditions.

There are annuals, too. Many of our North American deserts have large numbers of annuals, whose seeds lie dormant in the soil until a wet year coaxes them to spring into bloom. Notable among these are sand verbena (*Abronia latifolia*), *Verbena wrightii*, Dahlberg daisy (*Dyssodia tenuifolia*), California poppies (*Eschscholzia,* and many other poppies, as well), *Mimulus cusickii* (Desert monkey flower), *Phacelia campanularia* (bright blue bell-flowered scorpion flower), and *Baileya* species (a yellow desert daisy). Depending on your time and your budget, you may want to let the annuals in your xeric garden self sow, or you may want to purchase them each year and plant them. If you go for the self-sowing option, you can merely remove the seedlings where they don't fit into your plan.

The swordlike leaves of *Yucca schottii* mingle with blanketflower (*Gaillardia*) and Mexican hair grass (*Stipa*).

# CHAPTER 6

# SHRUBLIKE SELECTIONS

**ABOVE:** *Yucca rostrata* has the best cool blue foliage. This one's a young plant still, and hasn't yet formed a trunk. It's surrounded by the bright oranges of butterfly weed (*Asclepias tuberosa*).

**RIGHT:** *Yucca baileyi* needs no other reason to exist but its unbelievable symmetry. Use it to fill a large space, to give a backdrop to dryland annuals and perennials, or even as a traffic barrier.

Most gardeners think of shrubs as woody plants with multiple stems or trunks. Often they are as wide as they are tall, bushy, rounded, or vase-shaped, usually fine-textured with small leaves. In the garden, they add mass and weight to the composition. Planted individually or en masse, they may provide cover for wildlife, serve as a windbreak, act as a foil for smaller plants, or present a backdrop for flowering plants.

Some succulents — yuccas, chollas, and agaves — can also be used like shrubs in the landscape. Yuccas, with their wide and rounded habit, are a natural. A few species, such as *Yucca thompsoniana* and *Y. rostrata*, even grow to be almost like trees — or at least like some dwarf palm trees with spiky leaves. They maintain their shape throughout winter's storms, as a shrub might do; they don't even lose their leaves. Their cousins the red Texas yuccas (*Hesperaloe*) have similar large, permanent shapes.

I hereby propose to consider chollas as similar to rosebushes in their design role. They can be as large as a tea rose, even in Zone 5, as long as they are grown with perfect drainage. They are certainly spiny enough to keep company with roses and to serve as barriers to foot traffic. Likewise, their multidirectional branching gives them the character of a shrub, occupying horizontal as well as vertical space. Sometimes they look almost human in their multiarmed forms, standing sentinel as protectors in the garden.

## FOCAL POINTS

The garden, as an artistic composition, can be enhanced by giving some plants leading roles and harmonizing others as our lesser actors, or more-modest players. In the landscape, the *tallest* plant is often one of the focal points. This plant may be surrounded by others descending in order as we move outward, the whole forming a group with considerable visual weight. A somewhat shorter plant, possibly two-thirds or one-third the height of the first, may pull the eye to a second corner of our garden composition. The third point of this visual triangle might be a large low plant or even a large rock.

Using succulents as focal plants of the garden is scarcely a new concept, especially in the Southwest. We have all seen pictures of towering variegated agaves, larger than an automobile; the heavily armed, monster saguaro cactus; and giant yucca trees soaring over the deserts of southern California and Arizona. The other focal point of such a scene might be the low peaks of the desert mountains; the khaki greens and yellows of yard-high, sere desert shrubs; the two-to-three-foot-tall clumps of *Opuntia basilaris*; a foot-high golden barrel cactus; or perhaps even the bleached head of a long-expired steer.

The tallest succulents in the northern parts of the United States are found in the woody lily group. These plants are technically succulent, but their flesh is not as watery as that of ice plants, sempervivums, or even cactus. Because they hold less water, they are also more cold-hardy. They can defy what seems to be a rule of the plant kingdom: No succulent plant can grow taller than a foot in a climate where temperatures stay below 20°F for several months. Yet yuccas extend their slender, fibrous leaves more than a foot above the frozen winter ground without suffering as much damage as their more fluid-filled kin. If we are seeking focal-point plants among the succulents, this is the group in which to look.

Remember that the plants that form your focal points will set the tone for the garden, and they will be the first plants noticed, so keep them looking good by giving them a little extra attention. Watch out for spider mites in hot, dry weather and spray them if necessary. Trim off any rays that are winter-damaged and turn dry and brown.

The shining white spines of *Cylindropuntia whipplei* 'Snow Leopard' glow in the light, matching winter's cold blanket in brilliance and contrasting with surrounding dryland perennials in spring.

## TREE YUCCAS

Some of the more southern yuccas have the ability to "grow up tall." They begin life as single rosettes, but the caudex (stem) elongates, the leaves growing ever higher up from the ground, leaving a trunk below, often with the leaves of previous years hanging downward like a grass skirt. The caudex can branch well aboveground, creating treelike forms with pom-pomlike rosettes of sharp leaves. Some reach more than 20 feet in height.

**ABOVE:** The long, filamented foliage of *Yucca elata* graces a Texas garden.

**RIGHT:** A wonderful mature specimen of *Yucca rostrata* anchors the center of this garden vignette.

Tree yuccas add drama and verticality to any garden, and focus the attention of the visitor upon themselves and any other plants grouped with them. These tree yuccas are now being mass-produced quite inexpensively by several nurseries in the Southwest, where they grow more rapidly than in northern climes. Others are collected on private property. If you buy large specimens, make sure they have not been illegally collected.

### ❋ Yucca elata

This species, commonly called the soaptree yucca, grows slowly up to 15 feet tall, often branching but also forming pups at the base. Individual leaves are up to four feet long and quite narrow. As the foliage dies, rather than fall off the plant, the dead, straw-colored leaves form a shaggy skirt along the trunk. Flowers are white with rose highlights. Zones 5 to 8.

### ❋ Yucca faxoniana

The largest of the tree yuccas that regularly survive Zone 5 winters is the dramatic and stout *Yucca faxoniana*, also known as the Spanish dagger. If you have a very large building or rock outcrop, consider using this species, which may grow slowly to 20 feet in height. It needs many years of hot summers to form a trunk. You would be wise to place it where it faces south or west and, if possible, to shelter it against a wall. Its broad leaves and heavily tousled head garner attention in every season and impart to the garden scene a tropical flavor. Its leaves are quite wide, perhaps three or even four inches at their widest part, making a most impressive plant. Of all the tree yuccas, *Y. faxoniana* has the longest leaves, up to 55 inches. Zones 5 to 10.

### ❋ Yucca rostrata

The bluest and fullest of the hardy tree yuccas, this species — often called beaked yucca — forms a very full and usually perfectly symmetrical pom-pom with hundreds of leaves. It is certainly hardy as far north as New York City and Denver. Each leaf is about two feet long. The trunk is covered with the fibers of previous leaves, creating a gray haze. Zones 5 to 11.

### ❋ *Yucca thompsoniana*

Quite hardy, especially in sunny climates but even in southern New England, Thompson's yucca takes some 10 to 15 years to reach perhaps six or seven feet tall. That may seem like a long time, but keep in mind that trees themselves also take awhile to mature. *Yucca thompsoniana* has a generally yellow-green cast that distinguishes it from *Y. rostrata*, and it seems to become more yellow in winter. I like its tendency to branch, bearing side rosettes or tufts of swordlike leaves in midair. Leaves are about 14 inches long. Zones 4 to 9.

*Yucca thompsoniana,* its foliage with more yellow highlights than *Y. rostrata,* is like a sunburst or green halo in the garden. Quite often it has several "heads" on a branched stem.

## SHRUBLIKE YUCCAS

Yuccas are well known in the United States, and although they are all similar in appearance, there are actually some 40 species, all native to North America. These plants are considered exotic and wonderful by many overseas gardeners who have not grown up taking them for granted. This group includes large and small rosettes of narrow, stiff, usually sharp leaves in large rosettes. They are evergreen or ever-silver.

These plants are so striking in their form that they are emblematic of the West, although several are really from the Southeast. Shrublike yuccas can be used as focal points of the garden or may be blended into a landscape. More and more species are found to be hardy into Zone 4 and northward, and more variegated forms are being discovered and introduced.

### ✺ Yucca baccata

This species, sometimes called datil or banana yucca, has stiff, dark green leaves, and its rosettes reach 18 to 36 inches tall (or more). The white flowers are borne in large panicles; fleshy, edible, banana-like fruit adds another dimension of novelty and a tropical tone. These plants become quite large, spreading into mounds of rosettes as wide as 15 feet across, and are an excellent choice for a large landscape. Zones 4 to 10.

True to its name, the banana yucca (*Y. baccata*) produces edible, banana-like fruits.

### ❀ Yucca glauca

This species is common from the Great Plains to the Southwest, and is probably the species that is hardy farthest north. Because livestock can't eat it, *Yucca glauca* — also called soapweed — becomes widespread in pastures that are overgrazed. Some ranchers despise it; most of us just take it for granted. There are many forms, some that are more silver, some that are greener. When the flower stalks appear, rising to three feet, often wide and full of large, fleshy, greenish-white flowers, it's as if many thick candles have appeared on the prairies and along rock ledges. Zones 3 to 10.

### ❀ Yucca flaccida

True to its common name, weakleaf yucca, the leaves of this Southeasterner are floppier and less sharp than those of the western species. Leaves are droopier in winter, but recover their turgor in summer. The selection 'Golden Sword' has a wide band of yellow variegation, a good complement to any yellow-spined cactus or yellow-flowered perennial. The selection 'Ivory Tower' has outward-facing blossoms rather than drooping ones, producing in full flower a dramatic statement in the dry garden or a perennial border. Very cold-hardy, this species has escaped in Wisconsin and other parts north.

In dry climates, it needs supplemental water. Hinting of the tropics, this plant makes a spectacular addition to the garden. Zones 1 to 9.

### ⚜ Yucca filamentosa

From the Southeast, this species boasts long, loose fibers at the leaves' edges, rosettes two and a half feet high to five feet wide. The cultivar 'Bright Edge' has yellow-striped leaves; 'Color Guard' has gold-centered leaves that brighten in midsummer and may show considerable red highlights in winter; the leaves also have many curly filaments (hence the species name). 'Variegata' has wide white

edges on the leaves. In dry climates, this species needs supplemental water. Zones 5 to 10.

### ⚜ Yucca rupicola

Also called rock yucca or twisted leaf yucca, this reassuringly substantial plant is well grounded, and as hefty as a seasoned Army veteran. Its broad, twisting, army green leaves are often edged with a translucent strip of yellow. Place it where the sun backlights it for extra effect, and use it anywhere yellow flowers will pick up the overtones of the plant. This species intergrades with its cousin Y. pallida, becoming bluer and losing

the margin of yellow until it becomes a pale, glaucous-leaved creature. In dry climates, this species may need supplemental water. Zones 5 to 10.

FAR LEFT: *Yucca glauca* has heavy yellowish flowers and glaucous blue foliage.

NEAR LEFT: *Yucca flaccida* 'Golden Sword' provides a stunning contrast to blue-leaved eryngium.

ABOVE: A striking statement in gold in the summer, *Yucca filamentosa* 'Color Guard' picks up lots of red tones to add to winter's decoration of the garden.

## AGAVES — SHORT AND STOUT

Usually shorter than yuccas in the North, agaves are also stouter. Most have sharp-pointed leaves, much as the yuccas do, and the inattentive gardener can be stung by them. But somehow they are more self-contained, more majestic, and easier to get around, if only because they are more compact. Yuccas are like a starburst of thin, swordlike leaves. Agaves, on the other hand, have thick, substantial, three-dimensional leaves, often as thick as they are wide, closely clumped and closely held. Agaves give weight to any garden composition, and many of them add a blue-green hue to your color scheme. They are always focal points, simply because their shape is so lovely.

Differentiated from one another by the shapes of the individual leaves that compose their rosettes, agaves are all blessed with impressive flower stalks. They carry great flat-topped bundles of fleshy flowers 6 to 25 feet skyward, like heavy candelabras held up into the heavens. They may take 20 or 30 years to bloom, and they may all choose to bloom when your garden comes under some special weather spell (not easily forecast by the gardener). They reproduce by "pups," offsets from shoot or root, and thus often live on past their flowering (like sempervivums, the rosette that produces a flower stalk dies). The genus probably evolved in the subtropics, as the greatest number of species is found there, so it's not

LEFT: This *Agave havardiana* is still a baby and will eventually triple in size. Meanwhile it cavorts with a nice selection of succulents.

RIGHT: *Agave neomexicana*, solid as the rock in front of it, "ties down" its corner of the garden.

surprising that tropical birds find agaves of interest. A friend of mine had a 23-foot-tall stalk of *A. neomexicana* one summer that was visited daily by a flock of Bullock's orioles that fed on the flowers (or the flower nectar — it was difficult to tell exactly from down below!).

### Agave parryi

Parry's agave has leaves up to a foot long, and as wide as six inches across. Flower buds are red, opening to creamy yellow, a bit smaller in general than those of *A. neomexicana*, only slightly more than an inch long. *Agave neomexicana* is sometimes considered a subspecies of *A. parryi*, and certainly they intergrade in nature. All of this makes it difficult to determine the "real" botanical name, but it doesn't really matter to most gardeners; just buy the forms that appeal to you. It is also important to note that many forms of *A. parryi* are not hardy in Zone 5, while most forms of *A. neomexicana* are. It would be helpful if nurserymen and gardeners could begin to identify the hardiest forms by cultivar names. Zones 5 to 10.

### Agave havardiana

With very wide leaves and black tips, the rosettes of Havard's agave are lower, fuller, and stockier than those of *A. neomexicana*. The flowers are also larger — spectacular! There are very old specimens of this species in Denver, Colorado (Zone 5b, but semiarid). However, many plants have been killed in the occasional extra-cold winter, or in sudden rapid temperature drops in early fall or late spring. Zones 6 to 10.

### Agave neomexicana

The leaves of this Southwest native (hence its common name, New Mexican agave) are up to four inches wide, up to a foot long, and uniformly blue-green to powder blue. The spines tipping each leaf are brown to black to gray, and in some forms are *very* striking. The spines along the sides of the leaves are retrorsely barbed, each barb arching backward; should one become embedded in the flesh of your finger, it would not come out easily. There are smaller teeth on the lower part of the leaves. The flowers, when they appear, are deep yellow to orange inside, reddish brown on the outside, and quite large, each up to two and a half inches long. This is the hardiest species of *Agave*. Zones 5 to 10.

### ❈ *Agave victoriae-reginae*

Generally hardy to Zone 6, some forms of Queen Victoria agave may be hardy even to Zone 5 in some years, if sited appropriately (south-facing and protected). Even sheltered in this zone, this species will usually be killed at some point by the coldest snaps of weather. Gardeners south of Zone 6, rejoice in your better luck! The leaves of this queenly plant, very dark green with white lines, are very stiff and regal, to six inches long, with a blunt shape. The terminal spines are small, sometimes with two lateral spines, but leaf margins are otherwise unarmed. This is a wonderful choice to grow as a houseplant; just move the pot outdoors for the warm season. Most sources consider this to be hardy only to Zones 7 to 10.

LEFT: *Agave victoriae-reginae* is surely one of the most magnificent species, with the bright markings on the leaf and leaf margin. It may occasionally be hardy in southern Zone 6, but is reliable only in Zone 7 and south. Grow it indoors in winter and bring it out for the summer.

RIGHT: Tall and narrower than most of its cousins, *Agave lechuguilla* hails from southwest Texas and is hardy to Zone 7.

### ❋ *Agave lechuguilla*

This plant, also known as shin dagger, pups with enthusiasm, forming impenetrable mats in the Chihuahuan Desert. Some forms are hardy farther north than Zone 7. Leaves are narrow and strap-shaped, and often have pale stripes. Zones 7 to 10.

### ❋ *Agave utahensis*

Another species that contains hardy forms is *Agave utahensis*, the Utah agave. Its four subspecies all have heavily toothed leaf margins, including the striking *A. u.* var. *eborispina*, with spines as long as three inches; *A. u.* subsp. *kaibabensis*, with large green rosettes to two inches across; and the gray-silver *A. u.* var. *utahensis*, with silver-gray leaves edged with small, blunt spines. The flower spikes are narrow, candlelike spires. Zones 5 to 10.

### ❋ *Agave toumeyana* subsp. *bella*

This striking plant, commonly called Toumey's agave, has six-inch-long, linear, dark blue-green leaves that are concave above in cross section. The foliage is beautifully marked with lighter green speckling. The plant makes mats of pups. Its inflorescence is *only* six to eight feet tall, with tubular yellowish-green flowers. *Agave parviflora* and *A. polianthiflora* are superficially similar (the latter boasting gorgeous red flowers). Zones 6 to 10.

# A FANCIER'S GARDEN

DOES A PARTICULAR GROUP OF SUCCULENTS TAKE YOUR FANCY? Many gardeners go through phases during which they fall in love with a group of plants. For some it is cactus, for some tiny rock garden plants, for others sempervivums. During the "crush" phase of the relationship, the gardener begins to collect as many varieties or species of the group as possible. Suddenly there are a hundred plants — one each of a hundred kinds. This presents a challenge of design in the garden. In holding beds, one can simply have rows of plants, each with their label, but that looks strange as a landscape feature. Because I, too, have a tendency to fall madly in love with new groups of plants and want to collect them all, I have developed some ways to work a collection into a landscape:

**Add some topography.** Raise the level of the garden, constructing some gentle undulations, to introduce a bit of variety. You can model the landform in miniature with a small box of moist sand before you begin. Once you have your soil mix delivered, you can shape it with a shovel and rake.

In addition to adding interest, topography also provides niches where you can grow a variety of plants with slightly different needs. It gives a bit of shade on the north side, a bit more sun on the south, and improves drainage at the top of slopes, while increasing moisture toward the bottom of each hill.

**Incorporate rocks.** These can give reason and a sense of permanency to such slopes, as well as providing interest and year-round structure. Rocks of all one type will look most natural. A few large rocks, either at the corners of the beds, or at the top of a ridge can be made to appear as if they belong there.

In nature, rocks provide shelter for nearby plants, and they can do the same in your garden. The rock slows the heating and cooling of soil, and its water run-off provides a little extra moisture for the plants at its feet.

**Group plants together.** Perhaps place a shrub next to a perennial, next to a ground cover. Site large plants with several small plants nearby. Whether you're collecting cactus or sedums, such groupings may be better looking than evenly spaced individuals.

**Use foliage groups or contrasts.** Place a dark green-leaved plant next to a gray-green one. Or make pools of the same color, such as a group of three white-spined cactus. And don't forget about mixing textures. Coarse, large forms contrast well with fine-textured ones: a heavy agave with a tumble of petite-padded *Opuntia fragilis* at its feet; the vase-like shape of *Sedum kamtschaticum* next to the fine leaves of *Sedum lineare* 'Yellow

Drops'; a clump of heavy jovibarba rosettes with the needle-like foliage of *Sedum rupestre* 'Angelina'.

**Add plants from outside the group.** Even though you know that a specific bed is to be primarily for your cactus collection, a few leafier xeric plants, such as agastaches and salvias, will go a long way toward relieving the tedium of too many similar plant forms. A lawn of ground-cover succulents would be enhanced by a strategically placed dwarf evergreen, yucca, or agave. Or you might try dwarf roses in a glen of sempervivums. Just use a bit of imagination, and choose plants that will accept the same growing conditions as your group of beloved plants.

**Label plants well.** For any collector, labeling becomes a priority and often a problem. Plastic labels may break or be taken by birds, squirrels, or children, but they are inexpensive and readily available. Rewrite plant names in pencil (surprisingly, more permanent than many permanent markers) before the existing print starts to fade. Metal labels on metal sticks may be visually prominent, but they are sturdy and last a long time. Either of these can be pushed all the way into the ground, to prevent fading by sun and weather. Rather than deal with labels at all, some gardeners choose to create a map of the garden in order to keep track of their plants.

LEFT: Hardy succulents are at home among dwarf evergreens and perennials in John Spain's Connecticut garden.

RIGHT: The contemporary design of Eve Thyrum's garden in Delaware successfully incorporates stone and sculpture, to make hardy succulents fit in.

## CHOLLAS

Chollas are the hardiest of the shrubby cactus, towering, bristling protectors of the garden, shielders from casual harm. There are many species and many more forms of these spiny cylindropuntias and their near relatives. They may be used to add height to a dry garden, and they're striking and persuasive deterrents to those who otherwise might trespass or cut across those tempting corners of lots. Cholla spines are really mean, some being retrorsely barbed (bent backward away from its tip). They hurt on the way in and must be torn out through the skin, sometimes with pliers. The reasonably cautious avoid walking into them just because of the way they look, and even the most reckless and fey hesitate the second time.

Many gardeners refuse to put something so aggressively self-protective in their garden. But others admire their sheer prickliness and ornery nature. They can be handled safely with a combination of long-handled tools and clamps, and if necessary with such materials as discarded carpet.

Some chollas may be pruned to a tree form, creating interesting, statuesque shapes. Others form low mats, offering serious and secure refuge to small animals and birds. Although most chollas are native to southwestern drylands, they seem to have unexpected cold-hardiness. Most of the plants described below have been grown as far north as Connecticut and southern Idaho. Excellent drainage is vital to their health in climates with 20 inches of rainfall or more per year. They prefer full sun.

### ☀ *Cylindropuntia imbricata*

Commonly called the tree cholla, this species may grow to six feet high, and is said to be a shy bloomer until it reaches three feet tall. The stems are dark green with prominent green ridges lengthwise on the joints. A dozen or more wicked spines, some almost hairlike, are produced at each node. The flowers are up to two and a half inches across, magenta with a boss of yellow stamens and bright white stigmas. This plant may live 20 years or more when well pleased with its environment. Branches will droop in winter but recover quickly in spring. Zones 5 to 10.

LEFT: *Cylindropuntia imbricata*, with its long, slender joints, creates a treelike form.

RIGHT: *Cylindropuntia whipplei* 'Snow Leopard' is glorious in fruit and bud.

### ✺ *Cylindropuntia spinosior*

This spiniest of the genus *Cylindropuntia* (as the species name indicates), the cane cholla has at each node seven or eight spines of approximately the same length. The stems are gray-green behind this armature and are a half-inch to an inch-and-a-quarter thick. The segments are 7 to 10 inches long, and the spiny branchlets are often lax (oriented downward in a curve). This species seems to branch less than most of the others. It often reaches seven feet in height and may need to be staked in winter, to prevent its breaking in the snow or ice. Zones 5 to 10.

### ✺ *Cylindropuntia whipplei*

Forms of Whipple's cholla include diminutive, 10-inch plants with thin clumps of sticklike stems as well as forms that are three feet in height with bright white spines. Flowers are greenish yellow and appear in late July. Zones 5 to 10.

### ❀ *Cylindropuntia leptocaulis*

With its narrow purple stems in the "brown" season (late autumn to early spring), this cholla has a lively aspect. Its long, yellowish spines are often just one to a node and are held straight out. This vase-shaped plant has many branches arising from the base. Its red fruits, which are retained in winter, earn this plant the common name Christmas cholla. It tends to bear less fruit in more-northern regions, however. Zones 5 to 10.

### ❀ *Cylindropuntia echinocarpa*

Commonly called the silver cholla, this plant has stems that are about as wide as a cigar and branches freely. There are four or five long ivory, yellow, or red spines and seven or more short spines at each node. Zones 5 to 10.

### ❀ *Cylindropuntia davisii*

With its arching stems, the golden cholla forms low, rounded clumps into which no human hand dares reach. One can almost imagine a kangaroo mouse sheltered there. Golden spines, warm in the winter sun, add to the peculiarly lovely effect. There are three or four long spines, and two short ones at each node. The segments are extremely brittle, and thus break off easily. This plant may grow to three feet in height; in the garden it may easily be broken by snow or animals (ouch!). Zones 5 to 10.

## ❋ *Grusonia clavata*

Admired for its ferocious white spines (actually, they say the spine sheaths are what's white, but I've never gotten close enough to dissect one), the club cholla is striking — some might say frightening — in any weather, with its heavy, sharp, shiny, broad-based spines bristling in every direction. It reminds me of some fortification from medieval times, far bristlier than a porcupine.

The club cholla (formerly a member of the genus *Cylindropuntia*) provides a bright and impressive spot in the garden. In the low or dwarf form, this botanical beast spreads about six inches a year and reaches about eight inches in height. The generic form is taller, though not necessarily fiercer. Flowers are pale yellow. Zones 5 to 10.

**LEFT:** The cheerful, berrylike fruits of *Cylindropuntia leptocaulis* are the reason for its common name, Christmas cholla. Here you can see the "old wood" of the older branches. This is an attractive, vase-shaped plant.

**RIGHT:** *Cylindropuntia davisii,* from West Texas, has stunningly beautiful golden spines. This is the selection 'Copper King'. Place it where it catches the backlight of the setting sun, and it will bring you joy.

## THE PRICKLY PEARS

Of all the plants grown in North American gardens, prickly pears must be the most controversial. They are similar in size and design value to dwarf shrubs or conifers, and they offer year-round interest in foliage and form. Why do some people adore them, while others shudder at the thought? Could it be a childhood memory of a bad encounter with spines? Of course, nobody wants to come in constant contact with the protective features of prickly pears. You can, however, learn to handle them and to be free almost immediately of any inadvertently obtained prickles. And prickly pears have their seductive charms, too. I am here to tempt you into growing at least a few to round out your sampling of succulents. They're on my list of "must-have" plants, and they should be on yours as well.

These plants have fascinating forms, swollen stems that look like leaves, leaves reduced to spines, and improbably beautiful flowers. The petals of the flowers are often papery, always glistening and showy. Even the spines have their own charm, once we get over our initial fear; they may be white, yellow, golden, cinnamon, red, or black. Their variety is fascinating, their arrangements differing widely from species to species and selection to selection. Once we learn to observe them without suspicion, we can see why so many gardeners enjoy them so much.

Prickly pears, the easiest kinds of cactus to grow, belong to the genus *Opuntia*, native only to the Americas. There are many species across the United States, some more tolerant of rainfall, some of heat and extended drought. They all prefer full sun, and most will grow and flower best when given excellent drainage. This can be provided by growing them on a natural hill or steep slope, or by building them a mounded garden bed. If you have more than 35 inches of rainfall per year, you'll probably want to add some proportion of gravel to your topsoil. Some gardeners grow these plants in beds with a full foot of pure gravel added to the top of the soil. Somehow the roots find their way

down into the soil. Cactus are not heavy feeders — that is, they don't need much fertilizer, if any. They do enjoy a gravel mulch over the soil, which keeps the topsoil from splashing up onto the pads.

There are some 300 species of *Opuntia*, but the following are the most widely available and will give you a good start if you are new to growing prickly pears.

### ❋ Opuntia humifusa

This is the most eastern prickly pear and thus the easiest to grow in moist climates. It is hardy from Montana to Massachusetts, to Texas and Florida. It is also a prolific

bloomer. Flowers are yellow, sometimes with a good bit of red towards the base; because the flowers don't vary much in color, not many selections are offered. Pads lie flat in winter and shrivel. This species spreads rapidly, requiring the gardener to remove some at least every few years in order to keep it within bounds. Zones 3 to 9.

### ❋ Opuntia phaeacantha

Also known as brown-spine prickly pear, *O. phaeacantha* is native to drier haunts from Texas to California and into northern Mexico. The flowers are typically yellow with some hint of orange, so there are

LEFT: *Opuntia aurea* partners with *Salvia* 'Hot Lips' and *Agastache* 'Acapulco' in a dryland garden.

RIGHT: If given a well-drained site, cactus can thrive even in regions with high rainfall. *Opuntia humifusa*, planted into a gravel bed, adds a western feel to this Pennsylvania garden.

many selections with colorful flowers. The pads have long spines, especially along the edges of the pads, with tufts of bristly glochids, sometimes as long as half an inch. Zones 5 to 9.

Plants grown under the name *Opuntia engelmannii* may be a form of *O. phaeacantha* and are among the hardiest to have large blue pads. There are many forms with only a few spines.

### ❋ *Opuntia polyacantha*

With its botanical name way too similar to *O. phaeacantha* for the comfort of most of us, the many-spined prickly pear is the most common opuntia of the western Great Plains, growing from North Dakota to Alberta, from Texas to Arizona. The pads are usually very spiny, with five or more spines at each areole. Flowers come in a wide variety of exotic and wonderful colors, resulting in many cultivated selections. It is very hardy in most forms, and it is easy to root and propagate. Zones 3 to 9.

*Opuntia aurea* is another species close to *O. polyacantha*, but it closely resembles *O. basilaris* (which scientists assure us is unrelated). It is almost spineless, as is *O. basilaris*, and so they are both often cultivated and selected.

### ❋ *Opuntia macrocentra*

Native to New Mexico, *O. macrocentra* turns the blue-gray color of cold steel in winter, with a faint overlay of red sheen. Usually this species has at least a few heart-shaped pads, widest at the far end of the pad and indented in the center. It holds on to its red fruits through the winter, which makes it very decorative in the landscape. Zones 5 to 8.

LEFT: *Opuntia phaeacantha* drapes over a rocky ledge in this New York garden.

RIGHT: The nearly spineless pads of *Opuntia basilaris* offer up glorious roselike blooms.

# OPUNTIA FORMS AND FEATURES

*OPUNTIA RHODANTHA 'WAVY GRAVY'*

*OPUNTIA CHISOENSIS*

*OPUNTIA MICRODASYS*

*OPUNTIA ROBUSTA*

*OPUNTIA FRAGILIS 'POTATO'*

The red Texas yucca (*Hesperaloe parviflora*) raises its coral candles and smoky foliage, with *Ballota* clumped at its feet.

## RED YUCCAS

Sometimes called red Texas yucca, members of the genus *Hesperaloe* are not precisely yuccas, although they are in the same family. Perhaps the most noticeable difference is that the flowers of hesperaloes are a glowing coral-red, unlike the whites and ivories of the true yuccas. (There are also selections with yellow flowers.) Hummingbirds love these flowers and are especially drawn to them in late summer and while on their fall peregrinations, when the juvenile birds leave their home territories and wander, feeding on their way south, before actually making the big southward migration. The leaves share the stringy filaments of yucca and are similarly arranged in basal rosettes, but they are a bit fleshier and a bit more lax, and tend to be darker green.

Hesperaloes begin to bloom in late spring or early summer, the tall spikes growing up and up to as high as 6 or 10 feet. Flowering starts at the lower end of the shoot, higher flowers opening over a period of time. Hesperaloes are very tolerant of heat and drought. The plants will live with very little water, but they look and bloom better with a soaking every two weeks in dry climates.

### ✻ *Hesperaloe parviflora*

In the landscape, this red Texas yucca looks superficially like a true yucca. The rosetted leaves grow to three feet long, as do many yuccas. Upon closer examination, however, the leaves have gray-purple overtones, especially in winter, which are not seen in yuccas. When planting both genera, you can use *H. parviflora* as the echo of a yucca form.

So why plant it at all, if it's so much like yucca? Because of the glowing, coral-red or yellow, thick, fleshy, tubular flowers, about three-quarters of an inch long, with small teeth at the open end, borne on long stalks as tall as 10 feet. The flowers appear from late spring to midsummer, even later under good circumstances. A related plant, *H. tenuifolia*, has narrower leaves and is less hardy. Zones 5 to 10.

### ✻ *Hesperaloe campanulata*

This is a smaller cousin of *H. parviflora*, six to seven feet tall in bloom. It has pink flowers that are bell-shaped, more wide open and smaller than those of *H. parviflora*. It is a plant of the Chihuahuan Desert and thus not quite as hardy. Zones 6 to 10.

### ✻ *Hesperaloe funifera*

This is a larger species, with leaf rosettes as much as 6 feet tall and flower stalks to 15 feet. The flowers are an interesting gray-green. Any plant so big will draw attention to itself, making it a striking focal point. Zones 5 to 10.

# LOOK TO THE LANDSCAPE

ONE OF MY FAVORITE GARDEN SCENES is a scattering of tall plants over a low lawn of very short plants, mostly under a foot tall. The natural landscapes from which this model is derived are called parklands or savannahs. In Colorado there are parklands where the short-grass prairie sloping up into the mountains of the Front Range begins to be accented with occasional ponderosas, usually well spaced out, coming in on north slopes, along ridges, in the draws where moisture is a bit more available. In northern Idaho there are wet meadows where lodgepole pines and spruce sprinkle the landscape. In southern Wisconsin, northern Illinois, and eastern Iowa, tall and ancient bur oaks dot the prairies.

Were you to re-create this feel in a garden of succulents, you might choose a few tree yuccas and scatter them artfully across the garden,

planting only low cactus, sedums, delospermas, and such as the ground covers among them. Or you might add rocks, mimicking the scattered rocks of the mountain moraine, the streaked low ridges of the volcanic malpais of northern New Mexico and parts of southern Idaho, or any rocky scene you have admired in nature.

We mustn't pine, here in the northern half of the continent, for the huge yuccas and cactus and the dramatic succulent scenes of the Southwest, yet we may be inspired by what has been accomplished there. There are cactus, which grow treelike, as we know from saguaros in Arizona and California. For a strong stimulus to your imagination when creating a succulent garden, it does no harm to visit Huntington Botanical Gardens in San Marino, California,

Lotusland in Santa Barbara, California, or the incredible scenery of Joshua Tree National Monument (see Resources, page 147).

Whether or not you have formal artistic training, gather the scenes of nature into your memory, photograph them, dream about them. Choose your favorites and include a few elements from them in your garden. I find that it is difficult to express or explain some of these ideas, yet they find their way into my gardens. Just keep looking and considering, keep tweaking the garden to look the way it pleases you, keep planting, prune judiciously, and you will reach a picture that appeals to you, the gardener. And that is the goal, isn't it?

The Living Desert, a botanic garden in Palm Desert, California, offers inspiration for succulent gardeners.

## DESERT CANDLES AND BEAR GRASS

There are a few lesser-known members of the woody lily group that can also be used in dry gardens as shrublike masses. The two genera described below are more airy and open than either yuccas or agaves, but still occupy a large amount of space. Neither is as heavy in the garden portrait, and the background they provide for other plants and their flowers is less substantial.

ABOVE: *Nolina microcarpa* has narrow leaves and long strings inside the rosette. Often, the tips of the leaves also have long strings attached.

RIGHT: At Peckerwood Garden in Texas, many woody lilies are used to create a garden full of similar, but not identical forms, achieving a unique rhythm. In the foreground is a well-grown dasylirion, with spined leaves.

### ❋ *Dasylirion texanum*

Often called sotols, these are easily distinguished from other members of this group by the spines along the margins of the long, narrow leaves, making them almost saw-like. The spines are protective in nature, pointed in two directions so that they readily inflict damage on creatures that pass too closely and too rapidly by them. The flowers are also striking and distinctive, very small individually but borne on a stalk up to 15 feet tall. The crowded, narrow panicles of cream or white drip from this "stem." Each plant bears either male or female flowers. Sotols don't "candle" (as their flowering is called) until they are many years old, however. There are many other species, but only *D. texanum* tolerates wetter, colder climates well. Zones 5 to 10.

### ❋ *Nolina microcarpa*

This agave cousin has olive-green leaves to half an inch wide, the edges curved inward and thus concave in cross section, the rosettes up to five feet tall. The tips of the leaves are split into tufts and may form long, fibrous strings that wave wistfully in the breeze. The tiny, papery flowers are pale yellow or whitish. Commonly called desert bear grass, it spreads slowly from underground stems, a new tuft appearing a little distance from the original rosette. This is the showiest species of the hardy group.

Another common name for the genus *Nolina*, devil's shoestring, points to a distinguishing feature of loose threads at the tip of each leaf, more pronounced in some species but usually easily recognizable. (Anyone with teenage boys in sneakers will recognize the syndrome.) Flowers make these simple to differentiate from dasylirions, because the inflorescence is a broad, branched panicle and the flowers are bisexual — the more normal situation in plants, with both male and female parts on each specimen. The flowers, when they appear, are tiny, on stalks to four feet high.

*Nolina lindheimeriana* has leaves slightly narrower than those of *N. microcarpa*, almost wiry, and the leaf tips do not form "shoelaces." *Nolina texana* has keeled leaves and the inflorescence is shorter than the leaves, snuggled down among them. Zones 5 to 10.

# CHAPTER 7

# PLANTING, PROPAGATION, AND CARE

**ABOVE:** The decorative fruits of *Opuntia phae-acantha* can be harvested for seed-starting.

**RIGHT:** In this North Carolina garden, *Nolina nelsonii* (marginally hardy in Zone 7) is given a protected spot among shrubs and perennials.

Most succulents are far from fussy. These plants are easy to grow, easy to get along with, even easy to take for granted! They will be happy in a wide range of soils, from clay loam to sand. Most will do well under an array of moisture conditions, from one side of the continent to the other, from the Canadian border well into the South and Southwest. They ask only for an appropriate location — most in the sun. They are largely gracious companions for other perennials, often playing lesser roles as ground covers and filler plants, stepping forward in bloom time or holding the stage with evergreen foliage in winter and at all times of year. Most require very little pruning or dead-heading. Even where they are a bit aggressive, succulents seldom overrun their neighbors and smother them. Some gentle guidance will restrain most exuberant sedums, and the fact that they are weakly rooted means that they can easily be removed with hoeing or even pulling. A bit of nutrition and occasional fertilizer will suffice to make them content. Succulents usually get by with whatever is provided to the garden in general and they seldom need be the focus of the gardener's attention.

## PLANTING THE SUCCULENT GARDEN

Plant succulents with the crowns at ground level; this almost always means planting so that the soil level in its pot ends up even with the soil level of the garden. Slide or gently tap a (nonprickly) plant out of the pot, catching it with your hand so that the crisp top isn't broken. Plants grown in pots should generally be "rooted to the pot" when you buy them — that is, when you tip a plant out of its pot, roots should be visible on the surface of the soil. If the plant roots are circling the inside of the pot, loosen them by gently squeezing and stroking them with your fingertips.

Carefully firm the plant into the soil with your hands, pressing around it so that the roots are in good contact with the soil. Water within a few minutes of planting — unless you are planting into very moist soil or the weather is rainy. Watering with a stream of water rather than a spray enables you to deliver enough water to settle the soil particles into place and remove any small air pockets created during planting. Keep in mind, though, that cactus should never be watered in. (See Special Care for Cactus, opposite.)

### Garden-grown Plants

If you are transplanting a garden-grown succulent, dig a hole at least a few inches greater in diameter than the plant's root clump. Lower the plant until the soil of the clump is at the same level as that of the garden soil. Water both the plant and the soil around it thoroughly, both to provide water for the torn rootlets and to settle the soil with the weight of the water, so that air spaces are reduced and roots are able to make direct contact with the soil. Water daily for a few days, then every third day for several weeks, until established. If it rains, modify this schedule accordingly. Take care not to plant in water-logged soils or to water so much that the plant is constantly in a puddle. The roots will drown if all the air normally in the soil is replaced with water.

Ice plants, woody lilies, portulacas, talinums, and cactus are warm-weather growers and will do best in most regions if planted after mid-May and before the middle of August. Sedums and sempervivums can be planted at almost any time of the growing season, although they may not settle in well during a hot spell or when the soil freezes every night.

**LEFT:** This lovely composition features *Cylindropuntia whipplei* 'Snow Leopard', *Opuntia aurea*, *Sedum reflexum* 'Blue Spruce', and *Delosperma* 'Kelaidis'.

**RIGHT:** The bright green new pads of an opuntia emerge from a mat of *Dracocephalum,* with butterfly weed (*Asclepias tuberosa*) and a tall verbena as backdrop.

### Special Care for Cactus

Cactus should not ever be watered in after planting, as they need time to establish callus tissue, a thickened type of tissue that seals the cactus so that it's less susceptible to rot. When you receive a cutting, allow it to rest about a week then just stick the plant firmly into the soil and walk away. If cactus are kept wet, they are quite likely to rot.

In general, cactus require drier conditions than most sedums and semps — in fact, they should really be grown only in pots or in xeric gardens. Many cactus are grown in mixes of bark and grit or scoria (lava rock), but I do not recommend adding organic matter to planting holes, ever. Where rainfall exceeds 35 inches per year, cactus will need a thick mulch of rough gravel, 2 to 14 inches deep. They can also be grown in beds covered with 12 inches of sharp sand. The roots seem to find their way down to nutritive soils, but they can't escape soil organisms when in contact with wet earth.

In dry states such as New Mexico, Colorado, Oklahoma, and Wyoming, no special soil preparation is necessary to grow most cactus. Rainfall is low enough, the sun intense enough, air circulation great enough (out here we call it "wind"), that cactus need no protection from moisture.

### Fertilizing

In moderate climates and good soils, sedums, delospermas, and sempervivums may not require any supplemental nutrition. Cactus, agaves, and yuccas are also low feeders. However, all may benefit from a bit of fertilizer. If you think your plants are looking

hungry — if they have widely spaced foliage, are reluctant to bloom, or just generally fail to thrive — consider giving them a foliar feed with a low-nitrogen (10-30-20) fertilizer (too much nitrogen encourages the plants to become overly plump, making them more susceptible to rot and to winterkill). Again, consider your specific garden conditions when deciding on fertilizers; in high-calcium soils, for example, you may need extra nitrogen but already have too much potassium.

Because the nutrients in most slow-release, pelletized fertilizers are released only during warm weather, such products are more beneficial to the warm-weather growers, like cactus and woody lilies, than to the cool-weather growers, such as sempervivums and sedums. Also, most of these products are available only in equal portions of nitrogen, phosphorus, and potassium. There is no need to obsess about how to fertilize, though. It's better to feed with any fertilizer than never to feed — unless, of course, you're gardening on a nutrient-rich soil already.

### Water

In areas of the country with more than 30 inches of rain per year, most succulents will not need additional water, with the possible exception of during the time of establishment immediately after they are planted. In drier areas of the country, or in a very tough spot, such as when a yucca is planted between a building and the sidewalk, additional water may increase the health of the plant and the blooming as well. Many succulents, from sedums to delospermas, will do well without any additional water over a wide range of conditions.

**ABOVE:** If plants fail to thrive, a dose of low-nitrogen fertilizer may encourage bloom. This *Sedum spectabile* 'Neon' is clearly happy with its conditions.

# PROTECTING SUCCULENTS FROM WINTER COLD

THE BEST WAY TO MAKE SURE YOUR SUCCULENTS SURVIVE THE WINTER is to choose species that are hardy for your region and give them well-drained soil. Once gardeners get hooked on these sweet, chubby plants, however, they're inevitably tempted to grow more-tender varieties that need special protection to make it through the winter.

## Outdoor Protection

Marginally tender plants will sometimes overwinter with a protective covering or simply with proper siting and drainage. In areas of the country that experience occasional drops below freezing in nighttime temperatures, only temporary cover may be needed. In regions with a true, sustained winter and several months of freezing temperatures, more-permanent protection is necessary.

Cover has its own challenges. Only a madman would try to mulch cactus with straw or leaves (as you might do with perennials), because the weight of the mulch, especially when snow is added, would break the plants. And picking the straw and leaves off the cactus in spring would surely drive a person to distraction! Also, most succulents are more susceptible to rot when they are covered.

**Row covers.** One method of protection is to use woven row covers (which are often used to extend the season of vegetables). I have seen pots of cactus covered by row cover suspended on a hoop frame. This treatment raises the average temperature around the cactus by slowing heat loss from the earth. It probably gives you an extra 10 degrees of warmth, and in some winters this can mean life or death for the plants. But if the temperature drops to subzero and stays

there, the row cover probably won't make a difference.

**Bushel baskets.** Remember them? These, and large plastic plant pots, offer some protection to agaves and such. I recommend using structures like these if you have the urge to wrap your beloved plants in burlap, as you would an evergreen. Without the baskets, the burlap would become entangled on the sharp points of the plants. However, these plants like sun in winter, not dark, so limit the number of weeks you cover them.

**Styrofoam.** You could try Styrofoam rose covers, if you can find them in the right shape. In the extreme Southwest, 32-ounce Styrofoam cups are sometimes used to temporarily protect the tips of columnar cactus when nighttime temperatures dip into the 20s. To protect the environment as well as your cactus, limit use of this material, and don't let these cups blow around the neighborhood or stay on longer than necessary.

**Well-drained soil.** The best outdoor protection for succulents, in my opinion, consists of preparing the soil to drain well, placing the plants on an appropriate slope facing south or west, and mulching with gravel.

## Succulent Houseguests

The surest way to overwinter succulents that aren't hardy in your area is to grow them in

*Agave 'Joe Hoak' summers on the patio in a pot.*

pots and bring them indoors for the winter. Most succulents make fine houseguests if they have a cool, sunny window and occasional water. Carefully inspect each plant for pests before bringing it indoors. In the spring, slowly acclimate the plants to the outdoors, a few hours at a time, to avoid stressing them with too much sun and wind. Or you can give them outdoor shade for a week or two before placing them in full sun.

## SOIL AND SITE

There are some plants that show a strong preference for one type of soil or another. Sandy soils are those with many relatively large particles of quartz (which we know as sand) and fewer smaller particles of clay. Clayey soils have much less sand and many, many tiny particles. If you mix a clayey soil in a glass of water, the water will become cloudy and stay that way for an hour or so. A similar mixing of sandy soil will result in most of the soil settling to the bottom almost immediately and many fewer particles remaining suspended; thus, the water becomes clear much faster. Fortunately, for lovers of succulents, most of these plants have no strong soil preferences.

This bed makes an excellent home for succulents and other plants that demand good drainage. The slope decreases the water held in the soil at the top; the gravel mulch keeps the crowns of the plants dry and free from splashed soil.

Whether your soil is sandy or clayey, many beautiful succulents will grow for you. Most succulents do, however, need excellent drainage to prosper. This means only that water should disappear rapidly from the surface of the soil and from the top 12 inches. Because succulents hold large amounts of water in their tissues, they are susceptible to rot when in contact with puddles or wet soils for long periods.

If you are starting with a very sandy or gravelly soil, you'll find that sedums, woody lilies, and cactus will grow willingly for you. Sand and gravel (unlike clay) can't retain many nutrients, so mix in some organic matter before planting. Sand alone, because its particle size attracts water, wicks water upward from wetter layers deeper in the soil. Even though it drains very quickly, it may not dry out. Watch to see how your soil behaves. Dig down at least once a week to see how damp it is six inches below the surface. After a while, you'll probably be able to tell how dry the soil is just by looking at it.

## Amending Heavy Soils

If your soil is clay-based and you want it to drain more quickly, you can add organic matter in the form of well-rotted leaves, well-rotted manure, peat moss, shredded coconut husks, composted grass clippings, shredded garden cullings, sawdust, or even composted wood chips. Just make sure that your source of organic matter is free of weed seeds and herbicides. The material should be well composted, so that it's not actively decomposing in the garden. Nor should it be "hot," meaning in the process of rapid,

anaerobic decomposition; the heat itself can damage plants. Also, compost that is high in nitrogen, like sheep manure, can chemically burn plants. If the material is well decomposed, it also won't be carrying microbial organisms that will infect or compete with your plants.

Alternatively, you can mix in large quantities of sand and gravel. If just a small amount of sand is added to stiff clay, or if your sand is full of small particles of silt, adding sand may actually make the clay *less* porous, because the small clay particles fill in around the larger sand particles and a denser mix is created. A mix of one-third clay loam, one-third sand, and one-third pea-sized gravel will result in a soil that does not retain excess water, and that's what these plants want. Add a generous sprinkling of quality humus and a bit of well-rotted manure and you'll have a soil that will grow almost anything well.

Gravel is used in damp climates by gardeners who really want to grow plants, like cactus, that simply can't tolerate excess moisture around their crowns. One gardener I know actually uses a foot-deep layer of gravel! Somehow the rootlets find their way down to the soil below, and damage from wet spells is minimized.

A mulch of fine or mixed-size gravel will protect the roots of the succulents from surface wet. It also prevents the soil from splashing onto the plants during heavy downpours, carrying with it soilborne diseases. Gravel mulches can also unify the look of the garden, and make it easy to weed. If you object to the appearance, try mixing different sizes of gravel or add larger rocks.

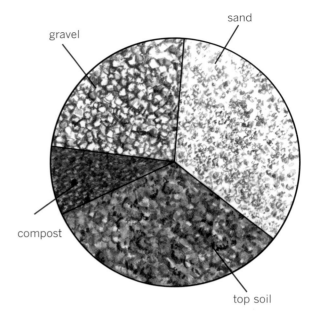

Good soil for succulents should contain almost equal parts gravel, coarse sand, and topsoil, with a healthy sprinkling of compost for good measure.

## Selecting the Site

Just as a water-saturated sponge will hold a large quantity of water when horizontal but shed water when held vertically, a sloped bed of soil raised above the level of the surrounding terrain will provide better drainage than the same soil in a level bed. Soil piled into a mound will drain even better. These kinds of sites are particularly suited to the culture of succulents. If you live in a region that receives a lot of rainfall and your yard slopes naturally in some places, site your succulents in these advantageous spots. If not, perhaps you can build a berm or a mound to provide a better home.

Select a sloping site to provide good drainage for succulent plants.

Pots give the best drainage of all — of course, I'm referring to pots with a hole in the bottom, not to solid-bottomed pots (also called cachepots). The small volume of soil loses moisture rapidly, just as small-bodied people (like children) lose heat faster than larger people. As an additional benefit, the soil in each pot can be modified to suit the needs of the plant in it. And there is no risk of earthworms blending the soil into the unmodified soils of the surrounding terrain.

## Sun

Sun is the most critical factor in promoting healthy and vigorous growth in succulents. And just because you can see your shadow, it doesn't necessary follow that you're standing in full sun. Full sun can mean that the plant is in sun all day long. It can mean that the plant is in sun throughout the calendar year. And it can mean that the sun is at a high angle, such as that provided by a south-facing slope.

The number of hours during which a plant remains in the sun is significant. Does the sun hit the plant only in early morning or late afternoon? Does the shade of trees dapple across the bed as the day progresses? Is there shade in winter? Higher altitude also means more powerful sun, because there is less atmosphere through which the rays must pass. To give succulents what they need, plant them where they get as much sun as possible, considering all these factors.

When I moved from upstate New York to Wisconsin, I noticed that we had more sunny days. When I moved from Wisconsin to Colorado, it became clear to me that the sun in Denver was more intense as well as a more frequent sight. Consult maps of solar insolation to see just how much sun power your region has.

A slope facing south actually receives more solar energy, as much as 40 percent more, than a north-facing slope. A west-facing slope will be the next best choice if you want to grow warmth-loving plants, such as cactus and woody lilies.

## Humidity and Air Circulation

Plants in the western half of the United States are accustomed to heat, but it's heat in the presence of low humidity. In the high humidity and high nighttime temperatures of the East in midsummer, some of the cold-weather growers may languish, even though they thrive on hot weather in the arid West. Succulents in particular can be susceptible to various forms of decay when they are surrounded by still, humid air. Perhaps because they have so much internal moisture, they can't ward off various forms of fungus and black spot.

Although you can't reduce the overall humidity in your climate, you can provide good air circulation, keeping moist air from settling around the plants. Air will move more freely down a slope. Keep trees and other plants pruned high above your succulents and away from them. Fences, especially solid ones, keep air from circulating through the garden. Know from which direction the prevailing breezes come and use this knowledge to direct the airflow across the perennial beds. Sound like too much work? You could select plants that just aren't that fussy — and there are many.

## PROPAGATION

Another joy of growing succulents is that you can so easily propagate them to expand your collection or to share. Because succulents have so much water stored in their bodies, pieces that break off can remain viable for some time, even without roots. Many are well adapted to produce roots readily from their leaves, stems, or, in the case of cactus, pads. Some root on their own after being broken off by animals, such as deer — and even gardeners!

Creeping sedums and ice plants are easily propagated from cuttings.

### Creeping Sedums and Ice Plants

To propagate any of these plants, take a cutting from one of the stems and tuck half an inch to an inch of it into the soil of a pot (or the garden), such that three to eight leaves are above the soil level. These are incredibly easy plants — no special soil is needed and many root in full sun or shade. I've rooted cuttings from one inch to eight inches long. Water as you would any plant in a pot until you see new growth. When the roots reach the edges of the pot, the cutting is ready for planting in the garden.

It is also easy to divide most sedums and ice plants by simply scooping out a small section of a clump from the ground and either replanting it in the desired location or potting it up. Talinums with more than a single taproot can also be divided in this way.

### Upright Sedums

To propagate an upright sedum, take a stem off the plant or cut off the tip of a stem. The cutting should be three or four inches long. Strip leaves from the bottom inch or two, then stick this portion into the soil. To speed up the growth of new roots, you can dip the

stem in a rooting hormone (either liquid or powder) first, although this is probably unnecessary. Water plants as needed.

Alternatively, divide an upright sedum into sections, shoots with roots, leaving at least three stems in each division. Plant into loose soil, keeping the soil at the same level at which the sedum was growing.

### Sempervivums

These are one of the easiest groups to propagate. I love making more plants of my hens-and-chicks! Just pull off a chick rosette and tuck the little stem into the soil of a pot. Firm down the soil. Often these rosettes will already be forming rootlets, giving them a jump-start into becoming new plants. Sempervivums are in most active growth in April and May, so this busy garden time is best for propagating them. Remember to label these immediately, as it will be difficult or impossible to identify them later.

### Cactus

Prickly pears and chollas are usually propagated by detaching with tongs a single pad, a stem, or a string of pads. (See Tips for

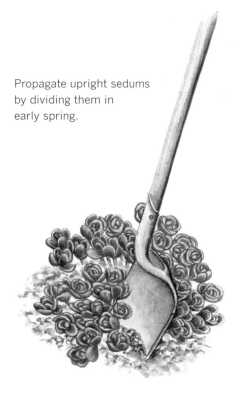

Propagate upright sedums by dividing them in early spring.

### Agaves and Yuccas

Agaves and yuccas can be divided by pulling the pups away from the mother plant and just planting them. If the pups are at some distance from the mother, just dig them up. These are pretty tough plants, so use a shovel if you need to. Try not to damage the mother plant, but it's okay to cut through the root tissue if necessary.

### Propagating from Seed

Some succulents aren't readily available, so you'll probably have to resort to growing them from seed if you're determined to have them. Cactus seed can be reluctant to germinate, and some must be washed in hydrogen peroxide before you sow them. Others will germinate only under warm and humid conditions, but once these have germinated, the seedlings must be moved into a drier location.

Lewisias and talinums are easy to start from seed. Sedums germinate readily from their very tiny seed too, but they are usually propagated by cuttings, as seed is not always available, at least for the more common varieties. Cultivars should always be propagated by cuttings, so that they retain the desired characteristics. Thus, most sempervivums are propagated by cuttings.

Agaves and yuccas can also be grown from seed, though they may take several years to develop into sizable plants.

Handling Cactus, page 142.) Leave these to dry out (in the sun seems to be fine, although shade is needed in very hot weather) and to form callus tissue over the wound, for a few days or a week. Then plant them in the ground or in a pot of well-drained soil. Bury one to four inches of the pad. (Even pads just left on the ground will sometimes take root.) Don't water them for several weeks.

Ball cactus are propagated by seed or by detaching a new ball or pup. With tongs, gently pull a pup away from its mother plant. Again, allow the wound to callus over, and then plant in soil or potting mix blended specifically for cactus. These mixes usually contain lots of gravel or volcanic gravel (scoria) and will open up the soil, to provide the roots with large quantities of soil oxygen and very sharp drainage.

ABOVE: Many agaves, like this *A. parryi,* can be propagated simply by pulling pups off the mother plant and potting them up.

# PLANTING CACTUS

CACTUS ARE PLANTS GENERALLY FROM AREAS OF LOW RAINFALL, and will not tolerate dampness at the roots over long periods. So if you garden where heaven grants you more than 25 inches of rain per year, you'll need to provide special conditions to grow cactus. Good soils for cactus range from the native clays in the Southwest where rainfall is less than 12 inches per year to mixtures of sand, gravel, and scoria where rain is 40 inches or more per year.

Some gardeners will want to build a raised garden, where the cactus forms can be viewed closer to eye level, and even sharper drainage is provided by a foot or two of quick-draining material such as half-inch to two-inch gravel, or even broken brick rubble, under the actual growing medium. Or you can grow cactus in straight sand, being careful to get a *sharp* sand, in which the individual particles don't pack too closely. Sand sold as "play sand" for sandboxes seems to be sharp; under no circumstances use mason's sand, which is fine and uniform. Remember that a slope also provides drainage: the steeper the slope, the sharper the drainage.

Choose a southern or western exposure for your cactus bed. If the bed slopes to the south or west, the soil will get more solar radiation, and thus stay warmer — at least when there's no snow! Cactus enjoy this, which is a nonscientific way of saying that they grow better with heat and intense sun. Perhaps damaging microbes don't grow as well in warmer, drier soils.

If you receive lots of rain, you could even provide an overhang or a structure for shielding the cactus from wet weather in spring and fall, whether it be a wide existing overhang of the house or a raised, remov-able sheet of Plexiglas. Cactus in particular will fall prey to rot in those early spring rains when the soil is frozen or very cold and water sits around the plants. Most don't mind rain in the hot summer months.

A gravel mulch will help keep the cactus plants dry at the crown. Some people use pea-sized gravel; some use much larger rocks, up to six inches across. Some gardeners use gravel 6 to 12 inches deep. Don't use any kind of organic mulch, such as bark or hulls, however — these materials will decay at the surface of the soil and the microbes involved in the decomposition process will be harmful to the cactus.

Provide nutrition by using a foliar spray or pelleted fertilizer; most cactus will grow well with just the nutrients already in the soil. You don't want to give cactus plants an excess of nitrogen, as they become too soft and are then subject to rot.

Some gardeners use strong fungicides and other chemicals to prevent rot and black spot in the cactus themselves. Be careful! If you choose this route, be sure to follow all directions on the product label. A better method is to try to achieve your results by changing the conditions of soil and exposure, rather than through chemicals. Forethought will save you lots of trouble in the long run.

Cactus, like this beavertail opuntia, benefit from the fast drainage a gravel bed provides.

137

## KEEPING SUCCULENTS NEAT

Most succulents are naturally neat, their plump stiff stems standing up without staking and looking tidy before and after bloom. They require scarcely any attention from the gardener — only occasional admiration. If you like a very neat look, you can trim sedums to the shape of a neat mound. Trim the spent flowers off the mats of sedums and ice plants, usually just below the inflorescence. Many gardeners opt to leave the flower stalks of yuccas, agaves, and hesperaloes through the winter, because of the drama created by their height.

Many cultivars of *Sedum telephium* need to be staked, especially when grown in regions that receive a substantial amount of rain or when planted in shady sites.

### Grooming Semps

Sempervivums send up short flowering stalks, and many gardeners enjoy the unusual look of the blossoms. If you don't, trim off the stalks just before they bloom. After bloom, the rosette will die. Pull out the flower stalk, holding the rest of the clump with the spread fingers of your other hand, if necessary. Fill the hole in the clump with a bit of fine gravel, or try teasing together the remaining rosettes gently with your fingers. Some sempervivum varieties bloom far more than others, so plant those that don't if you prefer their vegetative appearance.

In climates with low humidity, the outer leaves of the rosettes of sempervivums may dry out, especially in hot weather and in winter. Removing these leaves improves the appearance of the plants, but they are often sharp-tipped and will prick the fingers of the gardener. If they are dry enough, you can rub across the rosettes with a leather-gloved hand to remove many of the leaves. A pinch-and-pull action can work, too, and may be less painful after a rainfall or watering, when these leaves are a bit limp.

### Stopping the Spread

Restraining the spread of certain succulents may be a problem in some climates, and thus they may require some cutting back. If your creeping sedums spread too fast for your garden designs, merely cut off the edges of the mats with a spade, then lift, shake off the excess soil, and discard. Or give them to a friend, or perhaps transplant to a far-flung corner of the yard. Ice plants may be treated in a similar fashion, and so can ground-cover cactus.

Some sedums — *Sedum acre* and *S. hispanicum*, for example — regenerate from small sections of the plants, and these have given the whole group an undeserved bad reputation. The best way to control this kind of plant is never to introduce it in the first place. Should you inherit a garden where it roams, however, be especially diligent about containing it in spring and early summer. Hire a few children to go after it. Or try cultivating the soil weekly for a full season, hoeing out the little plants with a three-pronged cultivator, a stirrup hoe, or a short-handled hand hoe. You must also pick up the remains, and dispose of them in the garbage or compost. A wet/dry vacuum may work, too. If you want to compost the remains, make sure they are deeply buried, so they rot before they see daylight again.

If talinums seed too freely, they are easily pulled out. Sedums and ice plants rarely self-sow. Yuccas will self-sow in their home climates, and should be removed promptly if you don't want more.

Should yuccas and agaves sucker, eventually you may want to remove their pups. Choose a time when the soil is moist, in spring or right after a soaking rain. Some may require a pickax for complete removal, especially if you have a heavy clay soil.

### Staking

With most succulents, staking is hardly ever necessary. A few of the recent introductions of *Sedum spectabile* seem to be floppy, especially the varieties with maroon foliage. You could keep them upright with light bamboo stakes and ties or with metal peony hoops, or surround them with upright plants, like bee balms (*Monarda*), gas plants (*Dictamnus*), or chrysanthemums, between which they will be kept standing straight. Or just buy a better variety; many nonflopping ones have appeared in nurseries in recent years, such as 'Autumn Fire', 'Neon', and 'Carmen'. Flopping is usually an indication of too much water, too much shade, and too much food.

### COOL- VERSUS WARM- SEASON GROWERS

IT SEEMS THAT MOST SUCCULENTS have certain times of year when they grow most actively. I think of them as two groups — the warm-season growers and the cool-season growers. Sempervivums, for example, grow most (and most colorfully) in the cool months of spring and fall. During very hot weather, the bright reds usually fade to green and the rosettes seem to lie dormant. Propagators favor early spring for these plants, when a single rosette may grow as much in the month of May as in the entire remaining year. You will have comparable results in the garden.

Cool-season growers seem to appreciate a bit more water and a bit less sun than their more heat-seeking relatives do. Choose sempervivums for north-facing slopes. Lewisias also seem to grow well in cool weather, as do most sedums.

Cactus and the woody lilies generally grow most when nighttime temperatures are above 60°F. Similarly, they will want full sun, especially in the more northern parts of the country. In the far Southwest and South, a little shade may be appreciated, especially for young plants and smaller varieties. Other warm-season growers include most of the delospermas and talinums.

## WEEDING

Preventing weeds in new garden beds is easier than removing them once they're established. When you prepare a new bed, be sure to eliminate all grasses; don't turn over sod or leave bits of crabgrass in the soil. In theory, you could sift the soil and remove grass roots, but in practice, this does not work well. Better to cover the bed with black plastic for a hot month or two, or with old carpet for a whole growing season. Or you could use a grass killer. Avoid using manures and other composts that contain weed seeds.

In addition to providing good drainage, a gravel mulch helps suppress weeds.

Once established, most succulents will exclude many weeds, such as spotted spurge and most portulacas, as well as most weeds that seed themselves in, such as dandelions. Organic mulches — such as bark mulch, cocoa hulls, and grass clippings — will reduce weeds among succulents. I prefer shredded pine needles or pine straw because neither holds as much surface moisture. Gravel mulches are also effective, inhibiting the germination of weed seeds that require light to sprout, and these gravel mulches are more appropriate for those succulents that like really dry conditions.

### Getting the Grass Out

Grasses are probably the worst garden weeds. They creep in and are difficult to remove from any planting, but are especially annoying in mats and in the prickly havens of cactus. Prevention is most important in cutting down on garden labor. Use edging where the garden meets the lawn, then monitor the edge. Act rapidly to remove grass seedlings. Ruthless hand weeding is always my first line of defense, followed by a natural, vinegar-based spray.

If the grasses take over a large section of a succulent planting, you may try a weed killer that acts against only grasses and other monocots (although remember that yuccas, agaves, nolinas, and hesperaloes are monocots too; careful application is extremely important). Some succulents are resistant to such pesticides; for instance, if prickly pear cactus are healthy and growing well, they may not be harmed much by glyphosate but the grass around them will be killed. If the succulents themselves are under stress, they may die or become deformed. Keep in mind that some grasses are in full growth in early spring and late fall, because they grow at lower temperatures, and may be killed at those times with low doses of glyphosate. The succulents will not be in full growth at that time and may not be hurt, or not hurt as much.

If you decide to apply glyphosate on weed grasses, do so with caution. Lay newspaper

Weeding around spiky plants is best done from a distance — preferably with a long-handled hoe.

or plastic over plants you do not want to harm, then spray the grasses lightly with the herbicide. Wait until the herbicide has dried completely before removing the cover.

### Weeding Safely

Yuccas, agaves, and dasylirions are challenging to weed and clean around because of their sharp spines. It's a good idea to use safety goggles and long leather gloves when working near them. Try using a small-bladed, long-handled hoe to weed inside and under the yucca rosette. To remove leaves or blown-in debris, use long barbecue tongs, a long tweezer/forceps, a small-width leaf rake, or a long-handled trash-picker tool. Some leaf blowers can be used as vacuums also, and this might be a good time to use one.

Weeding cactus is best done with similar methods. Be careful! Consider planting cactus in large pots within the garden, making it easier to maneuver around them. Cactus do not usually require deadheading, thankfully, as the flowers almost seem to disappear as soon as they finish blooming. Cactus fruits are often as decorative as the flowers and need no removal, as they will shrivel and drop off by the end of winter.

When weeding cactus, you may be tempted to wear leather gloves. Keep in mind, though, that if you get cactus spines or glochids in the gloves, it will be difficult to remove them and you may never be able to wear the gloves again. In the end, although it may make you feel vulnerable, it is better to go bare-handed and use long-handled tools, like a dandelion digger, long tweezers, or even specially purchased cactus tools to pluck out "soft" weeds.

# TIPS FOR HANDLING CACTUS

*"Just don't touch 'em."*

— Kelly Grummons,
experienced cactus rancher and wrangler

To avoid having glochids embedded in your skin, it's best to handle cactus with tongs.

Long **forceps** are useful for handling cactus; hobby shops sell them to people who assemble delicate models of ships and airplanes. Medical-supply stores have them also. Or use **barbecue tongs.** For large cactus plants, such as chollas, medical equipment otherwise employed for delivering calves can be used! (Gardeners love their cactus but have learned to protect themselves at all costs.) Spines and even glochids easily penetrate leather gloves, which afford little protection. Once the gloves have glochids in them, they are useless — it is very difficult to get out all the stickers. (Also, many cactus spines will go through leather.) The better approach is to avoid having your hands come in contact with a plant at all.

If you get glochids in your skin, you can use **rubber cement** to remove them: just spread some over your skin, let it dry until it's sticky, and roll it off. The glochids should come off with the glue. Some folks recommend scraping (carefully!) over the skin with a single-edged **razor** — the tension apparently pulls out the glochids, rather than just cutting them off. Small numbers of prickles can be removed with good light, good magnification, a steady hand, and good **tweezers** (the kind with a broad tip, used for tweezing eyebrows, will be easier to use than the pointy-tipped one). Or you could try that handy and universal remedy **duct tape**! Just stick onto the affected part of the body, then rip off.

Avoiding direct contact with cactus in the first place is the best way to ward off trouble. Should you or someone you know actually fall into a cholla or a cactus patch, medical help may be required. Some cactus have toxins in the spines; some people are allergic. Beware! Never has respecting plants been so imperative! Some cactus spines must be removed with pliers or cut out of the skin.

A larger cactus plant can be moved or transplanted from pot to pot if you wrap it in a piece of old **carpet.** The spines won't readily pass through it. Discard the carpet afterward, of course!

## PESTS AND DISEASE

Succulents seem to appeal to many animals because of their crisp texture, or perhaps their water content, especially in dry climates. Animals may also break succulents by trampling them (deer and elk), digging for grubs or dens (skunks), or digging them up for unknown reasons (raccoons and squirrels). Could it just be curiosity?

Squirrels and other rodents can do damage to sempervivums especially. These animals seem to view the succulent rosettes as an artichoke-like treat. Rabbits will also munch the tips of sempervivums, or even spineless prickly pears, when little other food is available. Sedums and delospermas do not seem to be attractive, as far as I have seen. Sometimes birds will peck at sempervivums when they are first planted, pulling the unrooted plants out of the ground as they jerk upward with their heads. To protect semps, try the following: Cover the newly planted rosettes with hardware cloth or other screening until they become established. Or pin the rosettes in place with the snipped-off "elbow" of a wire hanger, or with a sod staple or landscape staple, pushing the wire firmly into the ground to hold down the root-ball. Push the wire all the way down onto the rosettes — the rosettes will grow up to conceal it. In the meantime, the plant will be difficult to pull or peck out.

### Disease
Most succulents are quite resistant to disease. In wet climates, cactus may need fungicide treatment to remain healthy. A deep gravel mulch, well-drained soil, and good air circulation around the foliage are the best preventive measures.

When planting sempervivums, you may choose to anchor them into the ground with a sod staple until their roots are established.

# REFERENCE MAPS

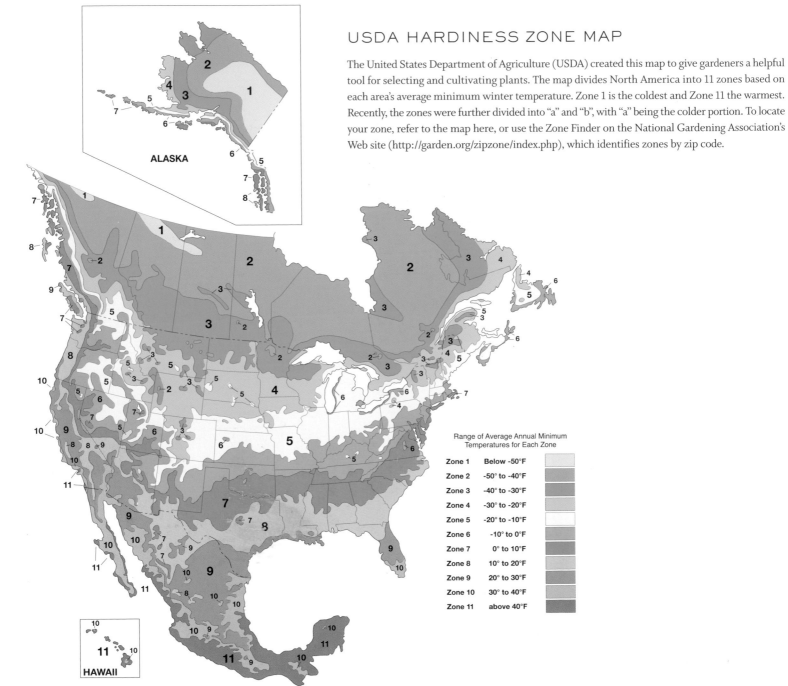

## USDA HARDINESS ZONE MAP

The United States Department of Agriculture (USDA) created this map to give gardeners a helpful tool for selecting and cultivating plants. The map divides North America into 11 zones based on each area's average minimum winter temperature. Zone 1 is the coldest and Zone 11 the warmest. Recently, the zones were further divided into "a" and "b", with "a" being the colder portion. To locate your zone, refer to the map here, or use the Zone Finder on the National Gardening Association's Web site (http://garden.org/zipzone/index.php), which identifies zones by zip code.

**ALASKA**

**HAWAII**

### Range of Average Annual Minimum Temperatures for Each Zone

| | |
|---|---|
| Zone 1 | Below -50°F |
| Zone 2 | -50° to -40°F |
| Zone 3 | -40° to -30°F |
| Zone 4 | -30° to -20°F |
| Zone 5 | -20° to -10°F |
| Zone 6 | -10° to 0°F |
| Zone 7 | 0° to 10°F |
| Zone 8 | 10° to 20°F |
| Zone 9 | 20° to 30°F |
| Zone 10 | 30° to 40°F |
| Zone 11 | above 40°F |

## SOLAR INSOLATION MAP OF
## THE UNITED STATES AND CANADA

This map shows the amount of radiation from the sun received by various areas of the North American continent. The amount of sun available to plants influences their growth and their health, since they use this light to produce their food for growth. Note that areas with higher rainfall get less sunshine, a natural consequence of both clouds and moisture in the atmosphere blocking the sun's rays.

While many plants are limited in where they can grow by the coldest winter temperatures, other plants need high levels of sunshine. Cactus, in particular, along with many plants originally from the Mediterranean, prefer large quantities of sun. In less sunny climates they will benefit from the maximum number of sunlight hours, especially in summer. In high-sun areas, they may thrive even in light shade. Solar radiation may also keep certain disease organisms on the plants' surface in check, benefiting their health that way, too.

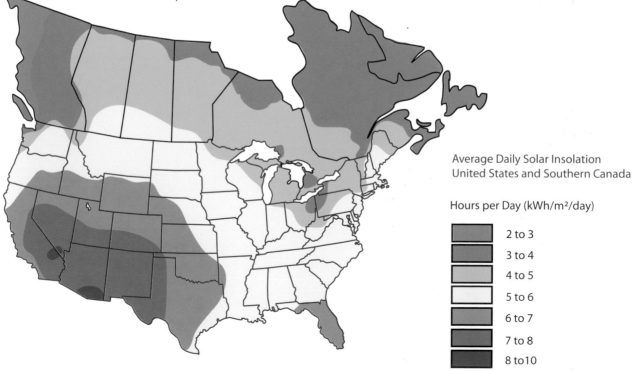

Average Daily Solar Insolation
United States and Southern Canada

Hours per Day (kWh/m²/day)

- 2 to 3
- 3 to 4
- 4 to 5
- 5 to 6
- 6 to 7
- 7 to 8
- 8 to 10

# GLOSSARY

**areole.** The area on a cactus stem that bears the spines or glochids; sometimes looks like a small dimple.

**aspect.** The direction toward which the ground slopes, as in "the north slope of the mountain could be said to have a northern aspect."

**calcareous.** Calcium-rich, or derived from limestone bedrock.

**caudex.** The stem–root axis of a plant.

**cultivar.** A selection of a plant from a wild or cultivated group of plants (within a species) that has desirable characteristics. A cultivar is usually propagated by vegetative means, such as cuttings. (Less commonly, a group of seedlings may be designated by a cultivar name and propagated by crossing a few individuals and maintaining a seed strain.)

**cyme.** A type of inflorescence characterized by flowers that bloom from the center outward or from the top of the flower stem down.

**flower segment.** A petal or a tepal (which looks like a petal, but may have originated as a sepal).

**foliar feed.** To apply a fertilizer to the surface of the leaves (as opposed to the surface of the soil). One might use a granulated fertilizer dissolved by a hose-end sprayer or in a pressurized tank, or a liquid fertilizer, which is then diluted.

**form.** A subgroup within a species. Certain forms may be selected and propagated for horticultural use.

**full sun.** In the sun during all hours of daylight, with no tree or building shade. This means more hours in the summer than in the winter in the Northern Hemisphere. Note that the farther north you are, the longer will be the hours of summer daylight, the shorter the hours in winter.

**genus.** A taxonomic group of plants including one or more species. Plural is genera. The genus is the first name of the scientific name of a plant or animal.

**glaucous.** The surface of a plant characterized as blue-gray or sea-green, or being covered with a thin coat of bluish white, waxy material, which often rubs off easily. Many plums and apples are somewhat glaucous in the latter fashion.

**glochids.** Very thin, hairlike prickles borne at the areoles of a cactus.

**high shade.** Usually the shade of trees, where the lowest branches are at least 6 feet, often more than 12 feet, off the ground. This condition usually allows for good air circulation.

**intergrade.** To change gradually over space from one geographic variation into another.

**petaloid.** Petal-like.

**pup.** A vegetative offset, or propagule — the "chick" of a hen-and-chick (*Sempervivum*), for example.

**retrorse.** Pointed backward from the tip of a leaf or stem.

**scoria.** A lightweight gravel of volcanic origin that has been formed in the presence of gas bubbles. The texture of scoria is rough, sharp, and hard to the touch, and provides a roughened surface area that can hold moisture without keeping the roots wet.

**semiarid.** A climate with normal rainfall of less than 18 inches per year.

**solar insolation.** The quantity of radiation (light) from the sun that contacts the soil or a plant. This is increased on a south-facing slope and decreased on a north-facing slope in the same locality.

**species.** A naturally occurring taxonomic group of plants that reproduce among themselves. The species is the second name of the scientific name. (Plural is also species.)

**spine.** A sharp-pointed, highly modified leaf.

**substrate.** The soil, or that which underlies the surface of the ground.

**tender.** Not hardy, as in plants that die when exposed to hard frost (about 28°F) for more than a few hours.

**woody lily.** A member of the yucca, agave, and hesperaloe botanical family, sometimes called the subfamily Agavoideae of the Liliaceae, sometimes segregated into the Agavaceae.

# RESOURCES

## WHERE TO SEE SUCCULENTS

*Public Gardens*

### Zones 3 to 5

*Colorado*
**Denver Botanic Gardens**
Denver, Colorado
720-865-3500
*www.botanicgardens.org*

**Western Colorado Botanic Garden**
Grand Junction, Colorado
970-245-3288
*www.wcbotanic.org*

*Illinois*
**Chicago Botanic Garden**
Glencoe, Illinois
847-835-5440
*www.chicagobotanic.org*

*Michigan*
**Matthaei Botanical Gardens**
Ann Arbor, Michigan
734-647-7600
*www.lsa.umich.edu/mbg*

*Minnesota*
**Minnesota Landscape Arboretum**
Chaska, Minnesota
952-443-1400
*www.arboretum.umn.edu*

*Pennsylvania*
**Longwood Gardens**
Kennett Square, Pennsylvania
610-388-1000
*www.longwoodgardens.org*

**Phipps Conservatory**
Pittsburgh, Pennsylvania
412-622-6914
*www.phipps.conservatory.org*

### Zones 6 to 10

*Arizona*
**Boyce-Thompson Arboretum**
Superior, Arizona
520-689-2811
*http://cals.arizona.edu/BTA*

**Desert Botanical Garden**
Phoenix, Arizona
408-941-1225
*www.desertbotanical.org*

*California*
**Ganna Walska Lotusland**
Santa Barbara, California
805-969-9990
*www.lotusland.org*

**Huntington Botanical Gardens**
San Marino, California
626-405-2100
*www.huntington.org*

**Joshua Tree National Monument**
Twentynine Palms, California
760-367-5500
*www.nps.gov/jotr*

**The Ruth Bancroft Garden**
Walnut Creek, California
925-210-9663
*www.ruthbancroftgarden.org*

*Nevada*
**The Springs Preserve**
Las Vegas, Nevada
702-822-8344
*www.springspreserve.org*

*New Mexico*
**Living Desert State Park**
Carlsbad, New Mexico
888-667-2757
*www.emnrd.state.nm.us/PRD/LivingDesert.htm*

**Rio Grande Botanic Garden**
Albuquerque, New Mexico
505-768-2000
*www.cabq.gov/biopark/garden*

*New York*
**Planting Fields Arboretum**
Oyster Bay, New York
516-922-9200
*www.plantingfields.org*

*North Carolina*
**Sarah P. Duke Gardens**
Durham, North Carolina
919-684-3698
*www.hr.duke.edu/dukegardens*

*Texas*
**Chihuahuan Desert Research Institute**
Ft. Davis, Texas
432-364-2499
*www.cdri.org*

**Private Gardens**

Many states have local chapters of the **Cactus and Succulent Society.** Most of these hold garden tours as well as meetings, and you can see who is growing what in your area and under conditions similar to yours. To contact the society, visit www.cssainc.org. Also of interest is the **North American Rock Garden Society** and its chapters. Most of the members grow at least some succu-

lents, and you will likely find that, as hopeless plant fanatics, they grow many selections. Many NARGS chapters have garden tours as well. For more information, visit www.nargs.org.

A private residence in Middlebury, Vermont, hosts the **Vermont Experimental Cold-Hardy Cactus Gardens.** For an appointment, call 802-388-3268.

## PHOTOGRAPHY CREDITS

Saxon Holt wishes to thank the public gardens that often went out of their way to accommodate a photographer's shooting schedule: Denver Botanic Gardens; Grand Junction Botanic Garden; New York Botanical Garden; Stonecrop Gardens in Cold Spring, New York; Chanticleer, A Pleasure Garden, in Wayne, Pennsylvania; John Story and Meadowbrook Farm; John Fairey and Peckerwood Gardens in Hempstead, Texas; Tony Avent at Plant Delights Nursery in Raleigh, North Carolina; Ed Snodgrass at Emory Knoll Farms in Street, Maryland; Timberland Gardens in Arvada, Colorado; and Ruth Bancroft Garden in Walnut Creek, California.

Special thanks also to homeowners and gardeners Don Campbell of the Chinle Chapter of Colorado Cactus and Succulent Society, Joe Grusczak and Bill DeGraff, John Spain, Eve and Per Thyrum, Ron Haenni, Sandy Snyder, Kelly Grummons, Dan Johnson, Stephen Miles, Jerry and Mary Kern, Larry Junge, Jeff Moore, Patrick Anderson, and Les Olson.

# SUPPLIERS

Many succulents are available in local nurseries, although the variety will vary greatly. Nurserymen who love cactus may carry a few hardy species mixed in with many tender varieties. Here, it is important to know what you are after. In some cases, it may be easier to mail order from a source that provides descriptions with hardiness indicated.

Sempervivums are available in thousands of varieties, and it is difficult for a gardener who loves them not to collect them. However, it is quite easy for a variety to become separated from its proper name tag, and many nursery plants are inaccurately or casually named. For proper names, stick to reliable mail-order sources or individual collectors who are fanatic about proper naming.

## Agaves, Yuccas, Hesperaloes, Dasylirions

**Bob Smoley's Gardenworld**
352-465-8254
www.bobsmoleys.com

**High Country Gardens**
800-925-9387
www.highcountrygardens.com

**Plant Delights**
919-772-4794
www.plantdelights.com

**Yucca Do**
979-826-4580
www.yuccado.com

## Cactus

**Agua Fria Nursery**
505-983-4831

**Cactus and Succulent Plant Mall**
www.cactus-mall.com

**Cold Hardy Cactus**
www.coldhardycactus.com

**High Country Gardens**
800-925-9387
www.highcountrygardens.com

**Intermountain Cactus**
801-546-2006

**J & J Cactus**
405-737-1831
www.jjcactus-succulents.net

**Mesa Garden**
505-864-3131
www.mesagarden.com

**Miles to Go**
520-682-7272
www.miles2go.com

**Plantasia Cactus Gardens**
208-734-7959

**Rio Grande Cacti**
505-835-0687
www.riogrande-cacti.com

**Timberline Gardens**
303-420-4060

## Delospermas and Their Kin

**Bob Smoley's Gardenworld**
352-465-8254
www.bobsmoleys.com

**High Country Gardens**
800-925-9387
www.highcountrygardens.com

**Sunscapes Rare Plant Nursery**
719-546-0047
www.sunscapes.net

## Sedums

**Bluestone Perennials**
800-852-5243
www.bluestoneperennials.com

**Mountain Crest Gardens**
877-656-4035
www.mountaincrestgardens.com

## Sempervivums

**Mountain Crest Gardens**
877-656-4035
www.mountaincrestgardens.com

**Squaw Mountain Gardens**
503-637-3585
www.squawmountaingardens.com

## RECOMMENDED READING

Anderson, Edward F.
*The Cactus Family*
Timber Press, 2001

Barr, Claude A.
*Jewels of the Plains: Wild Flowers of
the Great Plains, Grasslands, and Hills*
University of Minnesota Press, 1983

Evans, Ronald L.
*Handbook of Cultivated Sedums*
Science Reviews Limited, 1983

Irish, Mary, and Gary Irish.
*Agaves, Yuccas, and Related Plants*
Timber Press, 2000

Spain, John N.
*Growing Winter Hardy Cacti in Cold,
Wet Climatic Conditions*
Self-published, 1997
Available from John Spain,
69 Bayberry Road
Middlebury, CT 06762

Stephenson, Ray
*Sedum: Cultivated Stonecrops*
Timber Press, 1994

# INDEX

Page numbers in **bold** indicate main entries; those in *italic* indicate photographs or illustrations.

mulch, 97, 131, 132, *132*, **133**, 137, *137*, 140, *140*

## N

*Nananthus*, 42

New Mexican agave. See *Agave neomexicana*

*Nolina* (devil's shoestring), 18

    *lindheimeriana*, 124

    *microcarpa*, 124, *124*

    *nelsonii*, 126, *127*

    *texana*, 124

North American Rock Garden Society (NARGS), 150

## O

*Oenothera* (evening primroses), 97

*Opuntia* (prickly pear), 19, **118–21**

    *aurea*, 73, *85*, *118*, 119, 120, 128, *128*

    *basilaris*, *85*, 101, 120, *120*

    *beavertail*, 137

    *chisoensis*, *121*

    *compressa*, 69

    'Coombe's Winter Glow', 84, 94, *95*

    *engelmannii*, 94, *94*, 120

    *fragilis*, 73, 113

        f. *denudata*, 69, *69*

        'Potato', *52*, *66*, *67*, 69, *121*

    *humifusa*, 69, *119*, **119**

    *macrocentra*, 120

    *microdasys*, *121*

'Peter Pan', *68*, 69

*phaeacantha*, 60, *60*, **119–20**, *120*, *126*

    'Dark Knight', *84*

*polyacantha*, 69, 120

*rhodantha* 'Wavy Gravy', *121*

*robusta*, *121*

*schweriniana*, 69

*violacea* var. *santa-rita*, 15, *15*

oregano. See *Origanum vulgare*

organic mulches, 140

Oriental poppies. See *Papaver orientale*

*Origanum vulgare* (oregano), 94

*Orostachys*, 14, **32–33**

    *aggregata*, 33

    *chanetti*, 33

    *erubescens*, 33

    *fimbriata*, 33

    *fusarei*, 33, *33*, 57, *57*

        (*O. boehrmeri*), 33

    *iwarenge*, 27

    *spinosa*, *32*, 33

        'Minutissima', 27

*Othonna capensis* ("little pickles"), 43

outdoor winter protection, 131

## P

*Papaver orientale* (oriental poppies), 94

partridge feather. See *Tanacetum densum* var. *amanum*

Peckerwood Garden, *96*, 124

*Pediocactus* (ball cactus), 19

    *simpsonii*, 36, 56

*Penstemon*, 39, 97

    *eriantherus*, 39

    *pseudospectabilis*, 94

    *virens*, 39

perennials

    cactus and, 94–95

    in xeric garden, 97

    See *also* structure for perennials

pesticides, 140

pest management, 143

*Phacelia campanularia* (scorpion flower), 97

*Phlox hoodii*, 39

*Physocarpus opulifolius* 'Diablo' (purple-leaved ninebark), 90

pinks. See *Dianthus*

plant hardiness, 15–17

planting succulents, 126–37

    cactus, 129

    fertilizer and, 129–30

    garden-grown plants, 128

    site requirements, 133–34

    soil requirements, 132–33

    water requirements, 130

*Polemonium* 'Brise d'Anjou' (variegated Jacob's ladder), 31, 93

*Portulaca*

    *grandiflora* (rose moss), 19

    *oleracea* (purslane), 19, 61

Portulacaceae, 19

pots. See containers

prickly pear. See *Opuntia*

private gardens, 148

propagation of succulents, 135–36

public gardens, 147

purple-leaved ninebark. See *Physocarpus opulifolius* 'Diablo'

purple smoke tree. See *Cotinus coggygria* 'Royal Purple'

purslane. See *Portulaca oleracea*

## R

red Texas yucca. See *Hesperaloe parviflora*

reticulate iris. See *Iris reticulata*

rock garden, 17, *17*, 41

rock yucca. See *Yucca rupicola*

rooftops. See green roofs

row covers, 61

## S

*Salvia*, 62, 97, 113

    *argentea*, 86

    'Blue Hill', 94, *95*

    *greggii* 'Wild Thing', 94, *94*

    'Hot Lips', *118*, 119

    *officinalis* (culinary sage), 94

    *sclarea*, 86

sand for cactus, 137. See *also* gravel mulch

sand verbena. See *Abronia latifolia*

# OTHER STOREY TITLES YOU WILL ENJOY

**Covering Ground,** by Barbara W. Ellis.
Creative ideas to landscape with hardworking and attractive ground covers.
224 pages. Paper. ISBN 978-1-58017-665-1.
Hardcover with jacket. ISBN 978-1-58017-664-4.

**Fallscaping,** by Nancy J. Ondra and Stephanie Cohen.
A comprehensive guide to the best plants for brightening late-season
landscapes.
240 pages. Paper with flaps. ISBN 978-1-58017-680-4.
Hardcover with jacket. ISBN 978-1-58017-681-1.

**Foliage,** by Nancy J. Ondra.
A eye-opening garden guide to the brilliant colors and textures of dozens of
plants, all chosen for the unique appeal of their leaves.
304 pages. Paper with flaps. ISBN 978-1-58017-648-4.
Hardcover with jacket. ISBN 978-1-58017-654-5.

**Grasses,** by Nancy J. Ondra.
Full-color photographs and illustrated plans for 20 gardens designed to highlight the beauty of grasses in combination with perennials, annuals, shrubs,
and other garden plants.
144 pages. Paper with flaps. ISBN 978-1-58017-423-7.

**The Homeowner's Complete Tree & Shrub Handbook,** by Penny O'Sullivan.
The new bible of tree and shrub selection and care, showing hundreds of
plant possibilities in full-color photographs.
384 pages. Paper. ISBN 978-1-58017-570-8.
Hardcover with jacket. ISBN 978-1-58017-571-5.

**Stone Primer,** by Charles McRaven.
The essential guide for homeowners who want to add the elegance of stone,
inside and out.
272 pages. Paper. ISBN 978-1-58017-670-5.
Hardcover with jacket. ISBN 978-1-58017-666-9.

These and other books from Storey Publishing are available
wherever quality books are sold or by calling 1-800-441-5700.
Visit us at *www.storey.com.*